FIDELIO

An Opera in Two Acts

Libretto by

JOSEPH SONNLEITHNER

Music by

LUDWIG VAN BEETHOVEN

With Successive Revisions by
STEPHAN VAN BREUNING
and FRIEDRICH TREITSCHKE

Vocal Score Revised by
GUSTAV F. KOGEL

English Version by
DR. THEODORE BAKER

With an Essay on the
Story of the Opera by
H. E. KREHBIEL

Ed. 620

G. SCHIRMER, Inc.

DISTRIBUTED BY

HAL•LEONARD®
CORPORATION

7777 W. BLUEMOUND RD. P.O. BOX 13819 MILWAUKEE, WI 53213

FIDELIO
AN OPERA IN TWO ACTS
CHARACTERS OF THE DRAMA

MARCELLINE, the Jailer's daughter	*Soprano*
LEONORA, under the name of Fidelio	*Soprano*
FLORESTAN, prisoner of state, Leonora's husband	*Tenor*
JAQUINO, turnkey and porter	*Tenor*
PIZARRO, Overseer of the prison	*Baritone*
FERNANDO, Minister of State	*Bass*
Rocco, the Jailer	*Bass*

Chorus of SOLDIERS, PRISONERS, and PEOPLE

The scene of the Opera is laid in Spain

K. auch k. k. pr. Schauspielh. a. d. Wien

NEUE OPER

HEUTE MITTWOCH DEN 20. NOVEMBER 1805
WIRD IN DEM K. AUCH K. K. PRIV. SCHAUSPIELHAUS AN DER WIEN GEGEBEN

ZUM ERSTENMAL

Fidelio

oder: *Die eheliche Liebe*

EINE OPER IN 3 AKTEN

FREY NACH DEM FRANZÖSISCHEN BEARBEITE [*sic*] VON JOSEPH SONNLEITNER
DIE MUSIK IST VON
LUDWIG VAN BEETHOVEN

PERSONEN

Don Fernando, Minister	Hr. WEINKOPF
Don Pizarro, Gouverneur eines Staatsgefängnisses	Hr. MEIER
Florestan, ein Gefangener	Hr. DEMMER
Leonore, seine Gemahlinn unter dem Namen Fidelio	Dlle. MILDER
Rocco, Kerkermeister	Hr. ROTHE
Marzelline, seine Tochter	Dlle. MÜLLER
Jaquino, Pförtner	Hr. CACHÉ
Wachehauptmann	Hr. MEISTER
Gefangene	
Wache. Volk	

Die Handlung geht in einem Spanischen Staatsgefängnisse einige Meilen von Sevilla vor

DIE BÜCHER SIND AN DER KASSA FÜR 15 KR. ZU HABEN
PREISE DER PLÄTZE

	fl.	kr.
Grosse Loge	10	—
Kleine Loge	4	30
Erstes Parterre und erste Gallerie	—	42
Erstes Parterre und erste Gallerie ein gesperrter Sitz	—	56
Zweite Gallerie	—	30
Zweiten Gallerie ein gesperrter Sitz	—	42
Zweites Parterre und dritte Gallerie	—	24
Vierte Gallerie	—	12

DIE LOGEN UND GESPERRTEN SITZE SIND BEY DEM KASSIER DES
K. AUCH K. K. NATIONAL-THEATERS ZU HABEN

Der Anfang um halb 7 Uhr

23ʲᵗᵉⁿ *May* 1814

IM THEATER NÄCHST DEM KÄRNTHNERTHOR

VON DEN K. K. HOF-OPERISTEN

ZUM VORTHEILE

DER HERREN SAAL, VOGL UND WEINMÜLLER

ZUM ERSTEN MAHL

Fidelio

EINE OPER IN ZWEY AUFZÜGEN

NACH DEM FRANZÖSISCHEN NEU BEARBEITET

DIE MUSIK IST VON

HRN. L. v. BEETHOVEN

PERSONEN

Don Fernando, Minister	Hr. SAAL
Don Pizarro, Gouverneur eines Staatsgefängnisses	Hr. VOGL
Florestan, ein Gefangener	Hr. RADICHI
Leonore, seine Gemahlin, unter dem Namen Fidelio	Mad. MILDER
Rocco, Kerkermeister	Hr. WEINMÜLLER
Marzelline, seine Tochter	Dlle. BONDRA D. J.
Jaquino, Pfortner	Hr. FRÜHWALD
Staatsgefangene, Offiziere, Wachen, Volk	

Die neuen Dekorationen sind von Herren ARRIGONI *und* SCHARRHAN, *k. k. Hoftheatermahlern*

. .

LOGEN UND GESPERRTE SITZE SIND AN DER K. K. HOFTHEATERKASSE

ZU BEKOMMEN. DIE FREYBILLETTEN SIND HEUTE UNGÜLTIG

Der Anfang ist um 7 *Uhr*

THE STORY OF BEETHOVEN'S OPERA

BEETHOVEN has been credited with saying that Mozart's "Zauber-flöte" was the first really German opera. The reference, of course, went to the music rather than the libretto of that fantastic and puzzling composition; yet it is an interesting coincidence, if nothing more, that it was the author of the libretto of "Die Zauberflöte" who gave Beethoven the commission to produce "Fidelio," the work which to the majority of minds to-day seems the first repository in its field of the characteristically German musical virtues. Emmanuel Schikaneder—singer, actor, playwright and theatrical manager—has long been represented as a sad scalawag and ribald rogue, and it may well be true that he bore no greater burden of moral principles than many another adventurer in the theatrical world; but he had personal qualities which endeared him to Mozart, intellectual which won him a respectable place among the writers for the Viennese stage at the turn of the eighteenth century, and at least sufficient moral character to enable him to play a prominent managerial rôle in the Austrian capital for many years. The period was one marked by a careless gayety and an intellectual frivolity of which the Vienna of to-day knows nothing; but this fact serves only to accentuate the seeming anomaly that Schikaneder should have commissioned Beethoven to compose an opera for the Theater an der Wien, of which he was manager in 1803, and approved Beethoven's choice of such a subject as that of "Fidelio." Schikaneder and Beethoven stand as antitheses to each other in all things. Schikaneder it was who wrote the nonsense-verses in "Die Zauberflöte," who first acted the clown *Papageno* in that fantastic show-piece, who pestered Mozart to tickle the taste of the *hoi polloi* with his music, and to point the way whistled to him some of the melodies which Mozart brought into immortal conjunction with the grand and impressive strains of the rest of the score. *A time-server*. Beethoven was as severe a moralist in art as in life. That Mozart had been able to compose music to such libretti as those of "Don Giovanni" and "Così fan tutte" filled him with painful wonder. He had serious views of the dignity of music, of the uses to which it might be put in the drama, and more advanced notions than he has generally been credited with as to how music and the drama were to be consorted. It may have been merely worldly wisdom, shrewd self-interest, which suggested to Schikaneder the desire to have an opera from Beethoven's pen; but there must have been other considerations, and those of a praiseworthy character, which led him to make a generous proposal to Beethoven and to approve the choice of a subject so different from the subjects of the other operas, plays and spectacles with which his name is associated. Obviously, he never thought of asking Beethoven to write to order, as Mozart had done for him. For that, at least, he deserves a kind remembrance.

It was early in the year 1803 that Schikaneder made an agreement with Beethoven for an opera. It is fair to presume that the success of Beethoven's oratorio which had been produced at the Theater an der Wien had much to do with the contract on both sides. It is possible that from the beginning Beethoven had his eye on the book which he eventually composed, though it is not plain what it can have been that directed his attention to it before the production of an opera in Italian on the subject in Dresden more than a year later. Some sketches which have been found, made in 1803, of music used in "Fidelio" throw no light on the subject either way. There was obvious sympathy between the story of sweet and abiding conjugal love celebrated in the story written by Bouilly and the nature and moral convictions of Beethoven. Public mention of the projected opera was made in June, 1803, but more than two months earlier Beethoven and his brother Caspar, who was looking after the composer's business affairs, took possession, under the agreement, of lodgings in the theatre-building. Summer and fall of 1803 were spent by Beethoven at Baden and Unter-Döbling, where the "Eroica" symphony occupied his mind chiefly. The next year, 1804, had scarcely begun when the theatre passed out of the hands of Schikaneder into those of Baron von Braun, and Beethoven was obliged to give up the lodgings which Schikaneder had provided for him in the hope, probably, that constant association with the theatre would keep his mind upon his work. The operatic project, however, suffered only a temporary check; Baron von Braun took Schikaneder into his service, and the contract with Beethoven was renewed. The libretto was placed in the hands of Beethoven for musical setting in the winter of 1804. It was a translation into German of a French libretto which had already done service twice—once in its original tongue, once in Italian. The first setting was made by Pierre Gaveaux (1761–1825), a composer of small but graceful gifts, who had been a tenor singer at the opera in Paris before he took up opera-writing. His opéra comique, "Léonore, ou l'Amour conjugal," was produced on February 19, 1798. On October 3, 1804, when Beethoven was already occupied with his operatic project for Schikaneder, Ferdinando Paër produced an Italian version of the same book at Dresden, called "Leonora, ossia l'Amore conjugale." Paër (1771–1839) was conductor of the opera at Dresden at the time; two years later he accompanied Bonaparte to Warsaw and Posen; he then went to Paris, where he became *maître de chapelle*, succeeded Spontini as Director of the Italian opera, shared the conductorship for a space with Rossini, and was forced to resign in 1827. The preparation of the German version of the book was entrusted to Joseph Sonnleithner (1765–1835), whose name looms large in the history of music in Vienna. He was one of Schubert's intimate friends, founder of the Gesellschaft der Musikfreunde, successor, in 1804, of Kotzebue as secretary of the Austrian Court Theatres, manager, and many things besides. Also, he was an energetic champion of German, and the translator of opera-books for Gyrowetz, Weigl, and others, including Cherubini, whose "Faniska" and "Deux Journées" were given in Vienna in the course of the composer's sojourn in that city while Beethoven was at work on "Fidelio." It was at Sonnleithner's house that Beethoven met his great colleague, whom he reverenced and admired above all contemporary composers, and to whose influence he frankly yielded himself. It may have been "Les deux Journées" that suggested the melodrama which forms so impressive a moment in the grave-digging scene in "Fidelio." Certain it is that in one of the sketch-books owned by Joachim there are hints of "Fidelio" music in significant conjunction with excerpts from a trio in "Les deux Journées" and Mozart's "Zauberflöte." An understanding having been arrived at with Baron von Braun, Beethoven resumed his lodgings in the Theater an der Wien and began working energetically at his opera. As was his custom, the work was laid out in the form of sketches which Beethoven took to the country with him for elaboration. An idea can be gained of the zeal with which he applied himself to his task from the fact that when he went to Hetzendorf in the early summer he carried with him one sketch-book of 346 pages, sixteen staves on a page, completely filled with suggestions for the "Fidelio" music. Among the sketches are eighteen beginnings of *Florestan's* great air. The score was finished, including the orchestration, in the summer of 1805, and on his return to Vienna rehearsals were begun. It was the beginning of a series of trials which made the opera a child of sorrows to the composer. The style of the music was new to the singers, and they pronounced it unsingable. They begged the composer to make changes; but he was adamant. The rehearsals became a grievous labor to all concerned. The production was set down for November 20, and two days before the time Beethoven wrote: "Pray try to persuade Seyfried to conduct my opera to-day, as I wish to see and hear it from a distance; in this way my patience will at least not be so severely tried at the rehearsal as when I am close enough to hear my music so bungled. I really believe that it is done on purpose. Of the wind I will say nothing; but —— All *pp*, *cresc.*, all *decresc.*, and all *f*, *ff*, may as well be struck out of my music, since not one of them is attended to. I shall lose all desire to write anything more if my music is to be so played. Altogether, it is the most distressing thing in the world." It is the familiar picture of the nervously irritated and always suspicious composer. The momentous 20th day of November came. It found Vienna occupied by the French troops, Bonaparte at Schönbrunn and the capital deserted by the Emperor, the nobility and most of the wealthy patrons of art. The opera was a failure. Besides the French occupation, two things were recognized as militating against its success: the music was not to the taste of the people, and the opera was too long. Repetitions followed on November 21 and 22, but they confirmed the decree of non-success.

Beethoven's distress over the failure was scarcely greater than that of his friends, though he was, perhaps, less willing than they to recognize such of the causes as lay in the work itself. A meeting was promptly held in the home of Prince Lichnowsky, and the opera taken in hand for revision. Number by number, it was played on the pianoforte, sung, discussed. Beethoven opposed vehemently nearly every suggestion made by his well-wishers to remedy the defects of the book and score, but yielded at last, and consented to the sacrifice of some of the music and a remodeling of the libretto for the sake of condensation. The principal musical numbers eliminated are said to have been an air for *Pizarro* with chorus, a duet between *Leonora* and *Marcelline*, and a trio for *Marcelline, Jaquino and Rocco.* The book was put into the hands of Stephan von Breuning, who undertook the task of reducing its original three acts to two.* When once Beethoven had been brought to give his consent to the proposed changes, he accepted the result with the greatest good nature; it is noteworthy, however, that when the opera was put upon the stage again, on March 29, 1806, Beethoven had been so tardy with his musical corrections that there was time for only one orchestral rehearsal. In the curtailed form " Fidelio" (as the opera was still called, though Beethoven had fought strenuously from the beginning for a retention of the original title " Leonore"), made a distinctly better impression than it had four months before, and this grew deeper with the repetitions on April 10 and subsequently; but Beethoven quarrelled with Baron von Braun, and the opera was withdrawn. An attempt was made to secure a production in Berlin, but it failed, and the fate of "Fidelio" seemed sealed. It was left to slumber in silence for more than seven years; then, in the spring of 1814, it was taken up again. Naturally, another revision was the first thing thought of, but this time the work was entrusted to a more practised scribe than Beethoven's childhood friend. Georg Friederich Treitschke (1776–1842) was manager and librettist for Baron von Braun, and he became Beethoven's collaborator. Although Treitschke was a scientist by profession—he was, in fact, an entomologist, and the National Museum at Prague was enriched by him with a collection of 2,582 butterflies—Beethoven appreciated his literary talents so highly that he applied to him for the text of a melodrama, and in 1814 and 1815 set two of his poems to music for the celebration of the fall of Paris and its occupation by the allied troops. The revision of the book was finished by March, 1814, and Beethoven wrote to Treitschke: "I have read your revision of

* As the opera is usually performed nowadays, it is in three acts; but this division is the work of the opera directors, who treat each of the three scenes as an act.

the opera with great satisfaction. It has decided me to rebuild the desolate ruins of an ancient fortress." Treitschke rewrote much of the libretto, and Beethoven made considerable changes in the music, restoring some of the pages that had been elided at the first overhauling. In its new form "Fidelio" was produced at the Theater am Kärnthnerthor on May 23, 1814. It was a successful reawakening. On July 18, the opera had a performance for Beethoven's benefit; Moscheles made a pianoforte score under the direction of the composer, who dedicated it to his august pupil, Archduke Rudolph, and it was published in August by Artaria. The history of the opera, interesting though it is in every one of its phases, need not be here pursued further than to chronicle its first performances in the English, French and American metropoles. London heard it first from Chelard's German company at the King's Theatre on May 18, 1832. It was first given in English at Covent Garden on June 12, 1835, with Malibran as *Leonora*, and in Italian at Her Majesty's on May 20, 1851, when the dialogue was sung in recitative written by Balfe. There has scarcely been a German opera company in New York whose repertory did not include "Fidelio," but the only performances known for many years were in the vernacular. A company of singers brought from England by Miss Inverarity to the Park Theatre produced it first on September 19, 1839. The parts were distributed as follows: *Leonora*, Mrs. Martyn (Miss Inverarity); *Marcelline*, Miss Poole; *Florestan*, Mr. Manvers; *Pizarro*, Mr. Giubilei; *Rocco*, Mr. Martyn. The opera was performed nightly for a fortnight, but lest that fact lead some one to rail against the decadent taste of this latter day as compared with the earlier, let it quickly be recorded that somewhere in the opera Mme. Giubilei danced a *pas de deux* with Paul Taglioni; and the ballet has never since been as popular in New York as it was in 1839.

Beethoven wrote four overtures to "Fidelio," and—so at least it would seem from some sketches made in 1806—at one time contemplated another which would have stood in relation to that known as "Leonore, No. 1," as "Leonore, No. 3" does to "Leonore, No. 2." The order of their composition is not indicated by the published numberings. "Leonore, No. 2" was composed for the original production in 1805. "Leonore, No. 3" is a revision of it made for reasons partly indicated in the preceding historical recital, and was written for the revival of 1806. For performances contemplated when German opera was introduced in Prague in 1806, after the Viennese revival, Beethoven wrote that which is now known as "Leonore, No. 1;" it was to be "easier" of performance. The Prague enterprise fell to the ground, however, and the overture remained unknown till after Beethoven's death. The manuscript formed part of his posthumous assets, and it was sold at public vendue with the rest of his property. Haslinger, the publisher, bought it, and brought it out in 1832 under the title "Characteristic Overture, in C, Op. 138." For the revival of the opera in 1814 (if evidence adduced by Nottebohm be accepted as convincing) Beethoven for a time contemplated revising it and changing its key to E. Instead, he wrote the overture now generally played before the opera, and known in the books as "Overture to Fidelio." Unlike all its predecessors this overture, which is in the key of E, makes no use of melodic material employed in the opera; it is a "curtain-raiser" pure and simple. " Leonore, No. 1 " makes beautiful use of the principal phrase of *Florestan's* air, " In des Lebens Frühlingstage," and is close in feeling to the drama, though not so near its warm, pulsating heart as Nos. 2 and 3, which contain the story of the play *in nuce*, the chief moments being the sufferings of the conjugal lovers, the dramatic episode of *Florestan's* rescue, and the frenetic rejoicings over their reunion. The climax in both is reached in the trumpet signal, which, in the drama, tells of the approach of the *Minister of Justice*. Apropos of this signal, though it is foreign to the uncritical character of these prefatory words, it may be said that the device adopted by the late Mr. Theodore Thomas and some other conductors, of having this call sounded louder the second time than the first, is without justification either from the dynamic markings of the composer or the dramatic situation from which it is borrowed. The trumpeter is supposed to be stationed on the ramparts of the prison, and there remains; he does not come nearer to the scene of action with the *Minister of Justice*, of whose approach he was instructed to give warning. Dr. Marx broke a lance in favor of the overture "Leonore, No. 1," in which he found a delineation of the state of happiness of the married lovers before the beginning of the tragedy, and which was therefore, he thought, an excellent introduction. Wagner's prose writings abound with allusions to the overture "Leonore, No. 3," which testify to a very high appreciation of it. In his "Kunstwerk der Zukunft," after asserting that the old-fashioned opera presented no form to the German musician comparable with the symphony, he says: "Fully to grasp my meaning, compare the broad and amply developed forms of a symphony by Beethoven with the music-pieces of his opera 'Fidelio.' You feel at once how cramped and hindered the master must have felt, almost nowhere able to reach the full unfolding of his power; wherefore, as if to launch forth all his fill of force at last, he threw himself with well-nigh desperate weight upon the overture, and made of it a music-piece of thitherto unheard-of significance and breadth." In his essay "On the Overture," he wrote: " Beethoven, who never got a fair opportunity to develop his tremendous dramatic instincts, seems to have sought to indemnify himself for the loss by throwing the whole weight of his genius into the field of the overture which lay at his disposal. This he did in order to create, in his own manner, out of pure tonal form, the drama which he so much desired, and which he now, being emancipated from all the petty additions of the playwright, permitted to grow up anew out of his gigantically magnified germ. No other cause can be attributed for this wonderful overture 'Leonore.' Far from being a mere musical introduction to the drama, it presents this drama more completely and effectively than does the play itself. It is not an overture, but the drama in all its puissance."

There is little outward action in "Fidelio," and its plot may be quickly rehearsed. Two years before the opening of the drama *Florestan*, a Spanish gentleman who had incurred the hatred of *Don Pizarro*, has been torn from the arms of his devoted wife, *Leonora*, and secretly incarcerated in a dungeon in the State Prison of which *Don Pizarro* is Overseer. The wife's suspicions having been directed to the prison, she disguises herself in male attire, and under the name of *Fidelio* secures employment of the jailer, *Rocco*. An inconsequential by-plot develops out of the circumstance that *Rocco* has a daughter, *Marcelline*, who falls in love with *Fidelio* and, in the hope of marrying the supposed youth, discards Jaquino, the turnkey of the prison, who is perpetually pestering her with marriage proposals. *Rocco* is fond of *Fidelio* and looks with favor on his daughter's inclinations, much to the dismay of his young helper, who dares not betray the true state of affairs lest all hope of delivering *Florestan* be frustrated. She is eager to win the full confidence of the jailer, having learned of a secret dungeon-cell which only he is permitted to enter and in which an object of *Pizarro's* special hatred is confined. In honor of the name-day of the king *Rocco* permits all the minor prisoners to enjoy the freedom of the courtyard, and is severely rebuked by *Pizarro*, whose fears have been aroused by secret information received from Seville that *Don Fernando*, the Minister of Justice, is on his way to investigate the affairs of the prison. To avoid the discovery of his maladministration and his crime against *Florestan*, *Pizarro* resolves to accomplish the death of his secret prisoner at once. *Rocco*, whom he approaches with a bribe, refuses to commit the murder, which *Pizarro* thereupon undertakes to do, ordering *Rocco* to open a concealed cistern in the floor of the dungeon so that the body of his victim may be hidden therein. *Leonora* manages to get permission to help him in the work, and in the deep gloom of the cell discovers her husband. The cistern is opened; *Pizarro* enters to assassinate *Florestan*, but desiring to gloat for a last moment over him, discloses his identity. He is about to plunge his dagger into the helpless man, when *Leonora* throws herself as a shield in front of him with the cry: "First kill his wife!" *Pizarro* falls back, but only for a moment; again he advances with dagger drawn, but this time *Leonora* meets him with the muzzle of a pistol: "Say one more word, and you shall die!" At this instant a trumpet-signal is heard, which according to *Pizarro's* instruction was to be sounded if a carriage were seen approaching from the direction of Seville. *Jaquino* enters with the announcement that *Don Fernando* is arrived, and *Rocco* shows the would-be murderer to the courtyard to receive punishment at the hands of the Minister of Justice. The re-united lovers pour out their hearts in an ecstasy of joy. In the square before the castle *Don Fernando* learns the story of Pizarro's crime, releases the prisoners, and joins the hands of the happy pair. All join in a chorus in praise of wifely fidelity and conjugal love.

H. E. KREHBIEL

Blue Hill, Maine, August 15, 1906.

INDEX

Fidelio.
Overture.

L. van Beethoven.

PIANO.

18108

4

6

18108

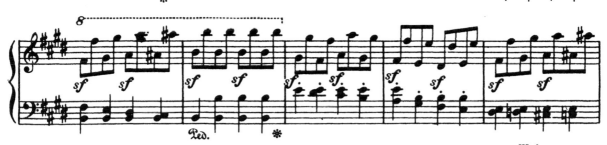

18108

Act I.

The courtyard of a State Prison.

Nº 1. Duet. „Jetzt, Schätzchen, jetzt sind wir allein."

(Marcelline is ironing.)

Jaquino (amorously, and rubbing his hands).

Jetzt, Schätzchen, jetzt sind wir al-lein, wir kön-nen ver-trau-lich nun plau-dern.
Now, sweet-heart, at last we're a-lone, There's time and a plen-ty to chat-ter.

Marcelline (continuing her work).

Es wird ja nichts wich-ti-ges sein, ich darf bei der Ar-beit nicht zau-dern.
I must work a-long till I'm done, 'Tis sure-ly no se-ri-ous mat-ter!

So
Go

Jaquino.

Ein Wört-chen, du Tro-tzi-ge, du!
Do hear me, don't be in a huff!

Jaquino.

Ich— ich ha-be—
I— I want-ed—

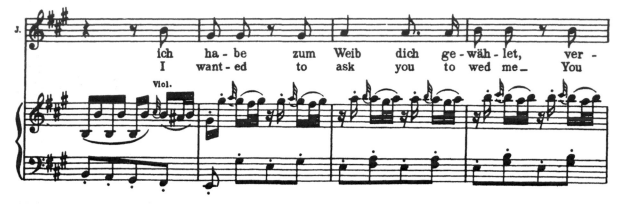

ich ha - be zum Weib dich ge - wäh - let, ver -
I want - ed to ask you to wed me— You

Marcelline.

Das ist ja doch klar!
Of course, that is clear.

stehst du? und—
fol - low? And—

und, wenn mir dein Ja - wort nicht feh - let, was
and then, if my heart's not mis - led me— What

M. So bin ich doch end-lich be - freit! Wie macht sei - ne

J. Thank good-ness, he must go a - way! O dear! from his *(aside)*

Hen - ker das e - wi-ge Po - chen, da war ich so herr - lich im

found it! they're knock-ing a - gain, now! *(aside)* My hopes nev-er yet were so

M. Lie - be, sei - ne Lie - - be mir bang, wie wer - den die

J. plead - ing, from his plead - - ing I'll die! How slow-ly the

Gang, und im - mer, im - mer entwischt mir der Fang, und im - mer ent -

high, And still she, still she a-voids a re-ply, and still she a -

M. Stun - den, die Stun - - den mir lang; ach wie wer - den die Stun-den mir

mo-ments, the mo - - ments go by, oh, how slow-ly the mo-ments go

wischt mir, im - mer entwischt mir der Fang, und im - mer, und im - mer, und

voids, and still she a-voids a re - ply,— and still she, and still she, and

M. lang; wie wer - den die Stun - den mir lang!

by, how slow-ly the mo - ments go by!

im - - - mer ent - wischt, ent-wischt mir der Fang! *(opens slide in door, receives pack-*

still— she a - voids, a - voids a re - ply! *age and lays it in his room)*

Marcelline.

18

Jaquino.

So— so wirst du dich nim-mer, nim-mer be-
You— you mean, that you nev-er, nev-er will

(aloud)

Du könn-test nun geh'n!
You're wait-ing here still!

keh-ren? was meinst du? Wie? dich
heed me? Do tell me! What? to

an-zu-seh'n, dich an-zu-seh'n, dich an-zu-seh'n, willst du mir
look at you, to look at you, to look at you, will you for-

Marcelline.

So blei-be hier steh'n!
Then wait, if you will!

weh-ren? auch das noch? auch das noch? Du hast mir so
bid me? Of all things! of all things! You've prom-is'd a-

18108

*'In other editions: geht zu weit!

Jaquino (geht, öffnet den Schieber, empfängt ein Packet und legt es in seine Stube). Wenn ich diese Thür heute nicht schon zweihundertmal aufgemacht habe, so will ich nicht Jaquino heissen. (Zu Marzelline.) Endlich kann ich doch einmal wieder plaudern. (Man pocht.) Zum Wetter! schon wieder! (Er geht um zu öffnen).

Marzelline (für sich.) Was kann ich dafür, dass ich ihn nicht mehr so gern wie sonst haben kann?

Jaquino (zu dem, der gepocht hat, indem er hastig wieder zuschliesst). Schon recht! Ich werde es besorgen. (Zu Marzelline vorgehend.) So. Nun hoffe ich, soll niemand uns stören.

Rocco (ruft im Schlossgarten). Jaquino! Jaquino!

Marzelline. Hörst du? Der Vater ruft!

Jaquino. Lassen wir ihn ein wenig warten. Also, auf unsere Liebe zu kommen —

Marzelline. So geh' doch. Der Vater wird sich nach Fidelio erkundigen wollen.

Jaquino (eifersüchtig). Ei freilich, da kann man nicht schnell genug sein.

Rocco (ruft wieder). Jaquino, hörst du nicht?

Jaquino (schreiend). Ich komme schon!(Zu Marzelline.) Bleib' hier, in zwei Minuten sind wir wieder beisammen. (Ab in den Garten.)

Marzelline. Der arme Jaquino dauert mich beinahe. Kann ich es aber ändern? Ich war ihm sonst recht gut, da kam Fidelio in unser Haus, und seit der Zeit ist alles in mir und um mich verändert.

Jaquino (goes, opens the slide, and takes in a package, which he lays in his room). If I haven't opened this door two hundred times to-day, my name is not Jaquino. (To Marcelline.) At last I can have another word with you! (Knocking.) Good gracious! so soon again! (He goes to open.)

Marcelline (aside). How can I help· it, that I no longer care for him as I used to?

Jaquino (addressing person who knocked, and hastily closing the slide). All right! I'll look out for it. (Coming forward to Marcelline.) So! Now, I hope no one will disturb us.

Rocco (calling from the garden of the castle). Jaquino! Jaquino!

Marcelline. Do you hear? Father is calling!

Jaquino. We can let him wait a while. Well, to go on with our love-affair —

Marcelline. Do go along! Father probably wants to inquire about Fidelio.

Jaquino (jealously). Oh, of course, one can't be quick enough, then.

Rocco (calling again). Jaquino, don't you hear?

Jaquino (screaming). I'm coming directly! (To Marcelline.) Stay here; I'll be with you again in two minutes. (Exit to garden.)

Marcelline. Poor Jaquino! I could almost feel sorry for him. But how can I change it? I really used to like him; then Fidelio came into our house, and since that time everything within me and without me is different.

№ 2. Aria. — „O wär' ich schon mit dir vereint."

was es meint, zur Hälf - te nur be - ken - nen! Doch
thought may be, But half___ she dare re - veal it. And

wenn ich nicht er - rö - then muss ob ei - nem war - men Her - zens - kuss, wenn nichts
yet, why should I blush to own A lov - ing kiss when we're a - lone, And none

(she sighs, and lays one hand on her breast)

uns stört auf Er - den _ Die
in sight or hear - ing! Sweet

Poco più allegro.

Hoff - nung schon er - füllt _ die Brust mit un - aus - sprech - lich
hope to - day my heart _ doth _ swell With joy _ no _ tongue can

Tempo I.

In Ru — — he stil — — ler
And when I wake with

Häus — — lich-keit er-wach' ich je — — den Mor — — gen, wir
ear — — ly day With-in our home so co — — sy, To

grü — ssen uns mit Zärt — lich-keit, der Fleiss_____ verscheucht die
lov — — ing words and la — — bor gay_ Ah, life_____ will all be-

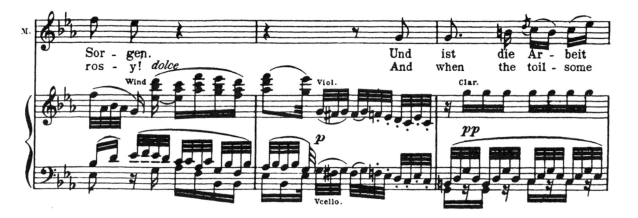

Sor — gen.
ros — y!

Und ist die Ar — beit
And when the toil — some

18108

★) Two other versions: glück lich glück - lich

Rocco (kommt vorn aus dem Garten).

Jaquino (trägt Gartengeräthe hinter ihm her und geht damit vorn in Roccos Wohnung ab).

Rocco. Guten Tag, Marzelline. Ist Fidelio noch nicht zurück?

Marzelline. Nein, Vater.

Rocco. Die Stunde naht, wo ich dem Gouverneur die Briefschaften überbringen muss, welche Fidelio abholen sollte. Ich erwarte ihn mit Ungeduld. (Während der letzten Worte wird an der Pforte gepocht.)

Rocco (enters from garden).

Jaquino (follows him with garden-tools, which he carries away into Rocco's lodge).

Rocco. Good morning, Marcelline. Hasn't Fidelio come back yet?

Marcelline. No, Father.

Rocco. It is almost time for me to take the letters, which Fidelio was to fetch, to the Overseer. I am awaiting him impatiently. (While he is still speaking, a knocking is heard at the gate.)

Leonore (ruft von aussen). Jaquino! Jaquino!

Jaquino (kommt aus Roccos Hause). Ich komme schon! (Er läuft geschäftig, um aufzuschliessen.)

Marzelline. Er wird gewiss so lange bei dem Schmied haben warten müssen.

Leonore (ist indessen zur Thüre hereingekommen).

Marzelline. Da ist er ja! Da ist er ja!

Leonore (trägt ein dunkles Wamms, rothes Gilet, dunkles Beinkleid, kurze Stiefel, einen breiten Gürtel von schwarzem Leder mit kupferner Schnalle; ihr Haar ist in eine Netzhaube gesteckt. Auf dem Rücken trägt sie einen Korb mit Lebensmitteln, auf den Armen Ketten, an ihrer Seite hängt eine blecherne Büchse an einer Schnur).

Marzelline (auf Leonore zueilend). Wie er belastet ist! (Sie nimmt ihr Taschentuch und trocknet ihr das Gesicht ab).

Rocco. Warte! Warte! (Er hilft mit Marzelline ihr Korb und Ketten abnehmen.)

Jaquino (im Vordergrund, bei Seite). Es war auch nöthig, so schnell aufzumachen, um den Patron da herein zu lassen. (Er geht in sein Stübchen, kommt aber bald wieder heraus und macht den Geschäftigen, sucht aber eigentlich Marzelline, Leonore und Rocco zu beobachten.)

Rocco (zu Leonore). Armer Fidelio, diesmal hast du dir zu viel aufgeladen.

Leonore (vorgehend, sich das Gesicht abtrocknend). Ich muss gestehen, ich bin ein wenig ermüdet. Der Schmied hatte an den Ketten so lange auszubessern, dass ich glaubte, er würde nicht damit fertig werden.

Rocco. Sind sie jetzt gut gemacht?

Leonore. Gewiss, recht gut und stark. Keiner der Gefangenen wird sie zerbrechen.

Rocco. Wieviel kostet das Alles zusammen?

Leonore. Zwölf Piaster ungefähr. Hier ist die genaue Rechnung.

Rocco (durchgeht die Rechnung). Gut! Brav! Zum Wetter! Da giebt es Artikel, auf die wir wenigstens das Doppelte gewinnen können. Du bist ein kluger Junge! Ich kann gar nicht begreifen, wie du deine Rechnung machst. Du kaufst Alles wohlfeiler als ich. (Bei Seite.) Der Schelm giebt sich alle Mühe; offenbar nur meiner Marzelline wegen.

Leonore. Ich suche zu thun, was mir möglich ist.

Rocco. Ja, ja, du bist brav. Man kann nicht eifriger, nicht verständiger sein. Ich habe dich aber auch mit jedem Tage lieber und – sei versichert, dein Lohn soll nicht ausbleiben. (Er wirft während der letzten Worte abwechselnd Blicke auf Leonore und Marzelline.)

Leonore (verlegen). O glaubt nicht, dass ich meine Schuldigkeit nur des Lohnes wegen –

Rocco. Still! Meinst du, ich könne dir nicht ins Herz sehen? (Er scheint sich an der zunehmenden Verlegenheit Leonore's zu weiden und geht dann bei Seite, um die Ketten zu betrachten.)

Leonora (calls from outside). Jaquino! Jaquino!

Jaquino (comes out of Rocco's house). Coming! Coming! (Runs with a show of zeal to open the door.)

Marcelline. He surely had to wait so long at the smith's.

(Leonora enters meantime.)

Marcelline. There he is! There he is!

(Leonora is clad in a dark doublet, red waistcoat, dark kneebreeches, low boots, a broad belt of black leather with a copper clasp; her hair caught up in a net-cap. On her back she carries a basket with provisions, on her arms chains; by her side hangs a tin box on a cord.)

Marcelline (hastens to Leonora). What a load he has! (Takes her handkerchief and dries Leonora's face.)

Rocco. Wait! wait! (With Marcelline he helps Leonora lay aside the basket and chains.)

Jaquino (in the foreground, aside). Faith, I had to be in such a hurry to let that fellow in! (Goes into his room, but soon comes out again and bustles busily about, keeping an eye, however, on Marcelline, Leonora and Rocco.)

Rocco (to Leonora). Poor Fidelio! this time you took too heavy a load.

Leonora (coming forward, wiping her face). I must admit, I am somewhat tired. It took the smith so long to repair the chains, I thought he would never be through.

Rocco. Are they well done, now?

Leonora. Certainly, they are well done and strong. None of the prisoners can break them.

Rocco. How much does all this cost together?

Leonora. About twelve piasters. Here is the exact bill.

Rocco (running through the bill). Good! Fine! I declare! On some of these items we ought to make at least double. You are a clever boy! I simply can't understand how you keep the bills down so. You buy everything cheaper than I. (Aside.) The rascal spares himself no pains — evidently on account of my Marcelline.

Leonora. I try to do whatever I can.

Rocco. Yes, yes, you're a good fellow. No one could be more devoted or sensible. I like you better every day I know you, and —you may be sure you shall reap your reward. (During these last words he eyes Leonora and Marcelline alternately.)

Leonora (embarrassed). O, do not think that I do my duty merely for the sake of wages!

Rocco. Hush! Do you think I cannot read your heart? (He appears to enjoy Leonora's increasing embarrassment, and then turns aside to examine the chains.)

№ 3. Quartet. – „Mir ist so wunderbar."

34

18108

*)Other editions:

-lo - se, o na -

Rocco. Höre, Fidelio, wenn ich auch nicht weiss, wie und wo du auf die Welt gekommen bist, und wenn du auch gar keinen Vater gehabt hättest, so weiss ich doch, was ich thue—ich—ich mache dich zu meinem Tochtermann.

Marzelline (hastig). Wirst du es bald thun, lieber Vater?

Rocco (lachend). Ei, ei, wie eilfertig! (Ernsthafter.) Sobald der Gouverneur nach Sevilla gereist sein wird, dann haben wir mehr Zeit. Ihr wisst ja, dass er alle Monate hingeht, um über alles, was hier in dem Staatsgefängniss vorfällt, Rechenschaft zu geben. In einigen Tagen muss er wieder fort, und den Tag nach seiner Abreise gebe ich euch zusammen. Darauf könnt ihr rechnen.

Marzelline. Den Tag nach seiner Abreise! Das machst du recht vernünftig, lieber Vater.

Leonore (vorher sehr betreten, aber jetzt sich freudig stellend). Den Tag nach seiner Abreise? (Bei Seite.) O, welche neue Verlegenheit!

Rocco. Nun meine Kinder, ihr habt euch doch recht herzlich lieb, nicht wahr? Aber das ist noch nicht alles, was zu einer guten, vergnügten Haushaltung gehört; man braucht auch — (Er macht die Gebärde des Geldzählens.)

Rocco. Listen, Fidelio! Even though I don't know how or where you came into the world, and even if you had had no father at all, I know what I am going to do; I—I shall make you my son-in-law.

Marcelline (hastily). Father dear, will you do it soon?

Rocco (laughing). Dear, dear, how jealous it is! (More seriously.) As soon as the Overseer has departed for Seville, we shall have more time. As you know, he goes once a month, to render an account of everything which has occurred in the State Prison. In a few days he must go again; and the day after he starts, I shall have you married. You may rely on that!

Marcelline. The day after he starts! Oh, Father dear, that *is* a sensible idea, sure enough!

Leonora (before greatly confused, now pretending to be glad). The day after he starts? (Aside.) Oh, what a new perplexity!

Rocco. Now, children, you love each other well and truly, do you not? But that is not all that goes to make a happy and well-ordered household; one also needs— (with a gesture as if counting money).

№ 4. Aria. — „Hat man nicht auch Gold beineben.‟

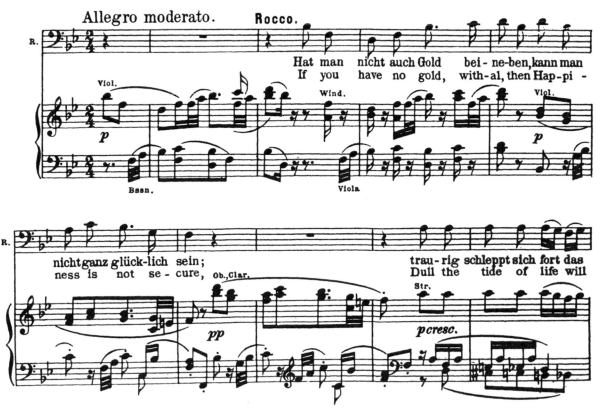

Le-ben, man-cher Kum-mer stellt sich ein, man - cher Kum-mer stellt sich ein.
crawl then, Man-y a care you must en-dure, Man - y a care you must en-dure.

Allegro.

Doch wenn's in den Ta-schen fein
But when you've a pock-et as

klin-gelt und rollt, da hält man das Schicksal ge - fan - gen, und Macht und
full as 'twill hold, Then fate will re-ward your ad - vanc - es, For Love and

Lie - be ver-schafft dir das Gold und stil-let das kühn-ste Ver-
Pow-er at - tend you for gold, Ful - fil-ling your loft-i-est

lan-gen, das kühn-ste Ver-lan-gen, und stil-let das kühn-ste Ver-lan-gen.
fan-cies, your loft-i-est fan-cies, Ful-fil-ling your loft-i-est fan-cies.

Tisch nur Lie - be fin - det, wird nach Ti - sche hung - rig sein, wird nach
dine on love when wed-ded, You'll be hun - gry when you're done, you'll be

Allegro.

Ti - sche hung - rig sein.
hun - gry when you're done.

Viol I.

Drum
And

läch - le der Zu - fall euch gnä - dig und hold und seg - ne und lenk' eu - er
so may the fu - ture bring plea - sures un - told, And may your good star nev - er

Stre - - ben; das Lieb-chen im Ar - me, das Lieb-chen im Ar - me, im
va - - ry! Your sweetheart be-side you, Your sweetheart be-side you, a

Beu-tel das Gold, so mögt ihr viel Jah - re durch - le - ben,
purse full of gold, Right long may your life be, and mer - ry!

so mögt ihr viel
Right long may your

Str.

Ob. & Bssn.

Leonore. Ihr könnt das leicht sagen, Meister Rocco, aber ich, ich behaupte, dass die Vereinigung zweier gleichgestimmten Herzen die Quelle des wahren ehelichen Glückes ist. (Mit Wärme.) O, dieses Glück muss der grösste Schatz auf Erden sein. (Sich wieder fassend und mässigend.) Freilich giebt es noch etwas, was mir nicht weniger kostbar sein würde, aber mit Kummer sehe ich, dass ich es trotz aller meiner Bemühungen nicht erhalten werde.

Rocco. Und was wäre denn das?

Leonore. Euer Vertrauen! Verzeiht mir diesen kleinen Vorwurf, aber oft sehe ich Euch aus den unterirdischen Gewölben dieses Schlosses ganz ausser Athem und ermattet zurückkommen. Warum erlaubt Ihr mir nicht, Euch dahin zu begleiten? Es wäre mir so lieb, wenn ich Euch bei Eurer Arbeit helfen und Eure Beschwerden theilen könnte.

Rocco. Du weisst doch, dass ich den strengsten Befehl habe, Niemanden, wer es auch sein möge, zu den Staatsgefangenen zu lassen.

Marzelline. Es sind ihrer aber gar zu viele in dieser Festung. Du arbeitest dich zu Tode, lieber Vater.

Leonore. Sie hat Recht, Meister Rocco. Man soll allerdings seine Schuldigkeit thun. (Zärtlich.) Aber es ist doch auch erlaubt, mein' ich, zuweilen daran zu denken, wenn man sich für die, die uns angehören und lieben, ein bischen schonen kann. (Sie drückt seine Hand.)

Marzelline (Roccos andere Hand an ihre Brust drückend). Man muss sich für seine Kinder zu erhalten suchen.

Rocco (sieht beide gerührt an). Ja, ihr habt recht, diese schwere Arbeit würde mir doch endlich zu viel werden. Der Gouverneur ist zwar sehr streng, er muss mir aber doch erlauben, dich in die geheimen Kerker mit mir zu nehmen.

Leonore (macht eine heftige Gebärde der Freude).

Rocco. Indessen giebt es ein Gewölbe, in das ich dich wohl nie werde führen dürfen, obschon ich mich ganz auf dich verlassen kann.

Marzelline. Vermuthlich, wo der Gefangene sitzt, von dem du schon einige Male gesprochen hast, Vater?

Rocco. Du hast's errathen.

Leonore (forschend). Ich glaube, es ist schon lange her, dass er gefangen ist?

Rocco. Es ist schon über zwei Jahre.

Leonore (heftig). Zwei Jahre, sagt Ihr? (Sich fassend.) Er muss ein grosser Verbrecher sein.

Leonora. That is easily said, Master Rocco; but, as for me, I assert that the union of two sympathetic hearts is the fount of true wedded bliss. (Warmly.) Oh, such bliss must be the greatest boon on earth! (Collecting herself, with more composure.) To be sure, there is something else which I should prize no less dearly, though to my sorrow I perceive that, despite all my pains, I am unable to gain it.

Rocco. And what may that be?

Leonora. Your confidence. Pardon me this gentle reproach; but so often I see you come up from the subterranean vaults of this castle quite out of breath and exhausted. Why do you not allow me to accompany you there, too? I should be so glad if I might help you with your work and share your toil.

Rocco. But you know I have the strictest orders to allow no one, whoever it may be, to visit the prisoners of state.

Marcelline. But there are altogether too many of them in this old fortress. You are killing yourself with work, dear Father.

Leonora. She is right, Master Rocco. Of course, one must do one's duty. (Tenderly.) But one may also be permitted, I fancy, to consider how one can spare himself a little for those who are his, and who love him. (She presses his hand.)

Marcelline (pressing Rocco's other hand to her breast). One ought to save oneself for one's children!

Rocco (moved, looking from one to the other). Yes, you are right, this hard work would be too much for me in time. True, the Overseer is very strict, but he must permit me to take you along into the secret cells.

Leonora (makes an impetuous gesture of delight).

Rocco. Nevertheless, there is one vault into which I shall hardly be able to take you, although I can rely upon you wholly.

Marcelline. You mean the one confining the prisoner of whom you have frequently spoken, Father?

Rocco. You have guessed it.

Leonora (tentatively). I believe it is a long time since he was imprisoned.

Rocco. It is more than two years.

Leonora (vehemently). Two years, you say? (Collectedly.) He must be a great criminal.

Rocco. Oder er muss grosse Feinde haben, das kommt ungefähr auf eins heraus.

Marzelline. So hat man denn nie erfahren können, woher er ist und wie er heisst?

Rocco. O wie oft wollte er mit mir von alle dem reden.

Leonore. Nun?

Rocco. Für unser einen ist's aber schon am besten, so wenig Geheimnisse als möglich zu wissen, darum hab' ich ihn auch nie angehört. Ich hätte mich verplappern können und ihm hätte ich doch nicht genützt. (Geheimnissvoll.) Nun, er wird mich nicht lange mehr quälen. Es kann nicht mehr lange mit ihm dauern.

Leonore (bei Seite). Grosser Gott!

Marzelline. Lieber Himmel! Wie hat er denn eine so schwere Strafe verdient?

Rocco (noch geheimnissvoller). Seit einem Monat schon muss ich auf Pizarros Befehl seine Portion immer kleiner machen. Jetzt hat er binnen vierundzwanzig Stunden nicht mehr als zwei Unzen schwarzes Brot und eine halbe Mass Wasser; kein Licht mehr [als den Schein einer Lampe] — kein Stroh mehr — nichts — nichts!!

Marzelline. O lieber Vater, führe Fidelio ja nicht zu ihm! Diesen Anblick könnte er nicht ertragen.

Leonore. Warum denn nicht? Ich habe Muth und Stärke!

Rocco. Or have great enemies; that amounts to much the same thing.

Marcelline. And so it has never been possible to find out where he came from, or who he is?

Rocco. Oh, how often he has tried to speak with me about all that.

Leonora. And? —

Rocco. It's best for a man in my place to know as few secrets as possible; and so I have never even listened to him. I might have blabbed, and I could not have helped him, anyhow. (Mysteriously.) Well, he won't trouble me much longer — he can last only a little while now.

Leonora (aside). Oh, my God!

Marcelline. Good heavens! how did he earn such severe punishment?

Rocco (yet more mysteriously). For a whole month, by Pizarro's orders, I have had to decrease his rations daily. Now, for twenty-four hours, he has had nothing but two ounces of black bread and a half-measure of water; no light [but a dim lamp], no more straw — nothing, nothing!

Marcelline. Oh, dear Father, do not take Fidelio down to him; he could not bear such a sight.

Leonora. Why not, then? I am strong and courageous.

№ 5. Trio. — „Gut, Söhnchen, gut."

gu - tes Herz_____ wird man - - chen Schmerz in die-sen
kind - ly heart_____ will shrink and smart____With-in those

Grüf - ten lei - den, dann kehrt zu - rück____
dark re - cess - es; Then, af - ter gloom,____

der Lie - - be Glück, der Lie - - be Glück und un-nenn-ba - -
true love shall come, true love shall come To cheer the heart____

- - - - re__ Freu - - den.
it bless - - - es.

Rocco.

Du wirst dein
Your hopes in

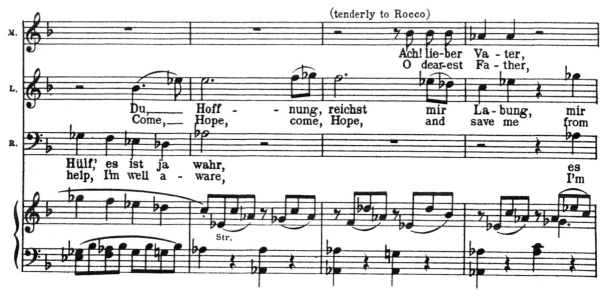

18108

Rocco. Aber nun ist es Zeit, dass ich dem Gouverneur die Briefschaften überbringe. (Marsch.) Ah! Er kommt selbst hierher! (Zu Leonore.) Gieb sie, Fidelio, und dann entfernt euch!

(Leonore giebt Rocco die Blechbüchse und geht mit Marzelline in das Haus.)

Rocco. But now it is time for me to take the letters to the Overseer. (March.) Ah! Here he comes himself! (To Leonora.) Give them here, Fidelio, and then off with you both!

(Leonora hands Rocco the tin box, and exit with Marcelline into the house.)

№ 6. March.

(Jaquino tritt aus seiner Stube und öffnet das Haupt-
thor. Während des zuvor begonnenen Marsches ziehen die
Offiziere mit den Soldaten ein. Dann kommt Pizarro.
Das Thor wird geschlossen. Jaquino trägt Korb und
Ketten in Roccos Wohnung.)

Erster Offizier (kommandirt.) Halt! Front!

Pizarro (zu dem Offizier.) Drei Schildwachen
auf den Wall! Sechs Mann Tag und Nacht an
die Zugbrücke, ebenso viele gegen den Garten
zu. Jedermann, der sich dem Graben der Festung nähert, werde sogleich vor mich gebracht!

Offizier. Gut, Herr Gouverneur!

Pizarro (zu Rocco.) Ist etwas Neues vorge-
fallen?

Rocco. Nein, Herr.

Pizarro. Wo sind die Depeschen?

Rocco (nimmt Briefe aus der Blechbüchse.) Hier
sind sie.

Pizarro (öffnet die Papiere und durchgeht sie.) Immer Empfehlungen oder Vorwürfe. Wenn ich auf
alles das achten wollte, würde ich nie damit
zu Ende kommen. (Er hält bei einem Briefe an.) Was
seh' ich? Mich dünkt, ich kenne diese Schrift.
Lass sehen. (Er öffnet den Brief, geht weiter vor, während
Rocco sich mehr zurückzieht.) „Ich gebe Ihnen Nach-
richt, dass der Minister in Erfahrung gebracht
hat, dass die Staatsgefängnisse, denen Sie vor-
stehen, mehrere Opfer willkürlicher Gewalt ent-
halten. Er reist morgen ab, um Sie mit einer Un-
tersuchung zu überraschen. Seien Sie auf Ihrer
Hut und suchen Sie sich sicher zu stellen." (Betreten.) Gott! wenn er entdeckte, dass ich diesen
Florestan in Ketten liegen habe, den er längst
todt glaubt, ihn, der so oft meine Rache reizte,
wenn er mich vor ihm enthüllen und mir seine
Gunst entziehen würde! — Doch es giebt ein
Mittel! (Rasch.) Eine kühne That kann alle Be-
sorgnisse zerstreuen!

(Enter Jaquino from his room; he opens the main
gate. During the march already commenced, the officers and soldiers make their entry. Then comes
Pizarro. The gate is closed. Jaquino carries basket and chains into Rocco's house.)

First Officer (commanding). Halt! Right face!

Pizarro (to the Officer). Three sentinels on
the rampart! Six men day and night by the
drawbridge, six others on the garden-side.
Let anyone approaching the moat be brought
before me forthwith!

Officer. Yes, sir!

Pizarro (to Rocco). Has anything new occurred.

Rocco. No, sir.

Pizarro. Where are the dispatches?

Rocco (taking letters out of the tin box). Here,
sir.

Pizarro (opening papers and glancing over them).
Always recommendations or faultfinding. If I
were to attend to all that, there would be no
end to it. (Stops at one letter.) What's this? This
writing looks familiar. Let me see. (Opens letter,
and goes further forward, while Rocco withdraws
somewhat.) "I have to inform you, that the Minister has learned that in the State Prisons of
which you are the Overseer several victims of
arbitrary power are confined. He begins his
journey to-morrow, to surprise you with an in-
vestigation. Be on your guard, and protect
yourself as best you may." (In consternation.)
Heavens! If he should discover that I have this
Florestan here in chains, whom he thought dead
long ago, he who so often aroused my ven-
geance — if he should unmask me before him,
and cause me to lose his favor! — Yes, there
is *one* way! (Quickly.) One bold deed can dis-
sipate all my fears!

№ 7. Aria with Chorus.—„Ha! welch' ein Augenblick!"

wühlen, o Won - ne, o Won - - - - - - - ne, gro - sses
wasted, Was rap-ture, was rap - - - - - - - - ture e'er so

Glück! Schon war ich, schon
great? Al - read - y, al -

war ich nah', im Stau - be, dem lau - ten Spott zum
read - - y in their pow - er, I saw the rab - - ble

Rau - be, da - hin, da - hin, ja, da -
glow - er And mock, and mock, ay, and

hin gestreckt zu sein! Nun_____ ist es mir ge -
mock me in my fall; Now_____ no-thing ill can

wor - den, den Mör - der selbst zu mor - den, nun ____
hap - pen, For Fate pro - vides my weap - on! Now ____

____ ist es mir ge - worden, den Mör - der selbst zu mor - den, den
____ nothing ill can happen, For Fate pro - vides my weap - on, for

Mör - der selbst zu mor - den!
Fate pro - vides my weap - on!

Ha! Ha! welch' ein Au - genblick! Die
Ha! Ha! It is not too late! My

Ra - che werd' ich küh - len! dich, dich ru - fet dein Ge -
ven - geance shall be tast - ed! You, you go to meet your

hin, da - hin ge - streckt zu my
mock, and mock me in my

sein! Nun, nun ist es mir ge -
fall; Now, now no-thing ill can

wor - den, den Mör - der selbst zu mor - den! In sei - ner
hap - pen, For Fate pro - vides my weap - on! When with his

letz - - ten Stun - de, den Stahl in sei - ner
death - - wound ly - ing Be - fore me, as he's

Wun - de, ihm noch in's Ohr zu schrei'n: Tri -
dy - ing, Still in his ear I'll call: Re -

66

18108

Pizarro. Ich darf keinen Augenblick säu - men, alle Anstalten zu meinem Vorhaben zu treffen. Heute soll der Minister ankommen. Nur die grösste Vorsicht und Eile können mich ret - ten. (Leise zum Offizier, den er mit einem Wink in den Vordergrund führt.) Hauptmann! Besteigen Sie mit einem Trompeter sogleich den Thurm. Se - hen Sie mit der grössten Achtsamkeit auf die Strasse von Sevilla. Sobald Sie einen Wagen von Reitern begleitet sehen, lassen Sie augen - blicklich durch den Trompeter ein Signal geben. Verstehen Sie augenblicklich! Ich erwarte die grösste Pünktlichkeit. Sie haften mir mit Ih - rem Kopf dafür. Fort! auf eure Posten!

Offizier. Gewehr auf! Marsch! (Soldaten ge - hen ab.)

Leonore (in der Thür lauschend).

Pizarro (zu Rocco.) He!

Rocco. Herr!

Pizarro (betrachtet ihn eine Weile aufmerksam, für sich.) Ich muss ihn zu gewinnen suchen. Ohne sei - ne Hilfe kann ich es nicht ausführen. (Laut.) Komm näher!

Pizarro. I have not a moment to lose in getting all in readiness for my scheme. The Minister is to arrive to-day. Only the utmost precaution and haste can save me. (Aside to the Officer, whom he beckons forward.) Captain! Go immediately to the top of the tower, with a bugler. Keep the strictest watch over the road to Seville. As soon as you see a carriage es - corted by cavalry, let the bugler give a sig - nal instantly. You understand me: instantly! I expect the greatest punctuality. Your head will pay the forfeit! Now, to your posts!

Officer. Shoulder arms! Forward march! (Exeunt Soldiers.)

(Leonora is listening in the doorway.)

Pizarro (to Rocco). Hey!

Rocco. Sir!

Pizarro (examines him awhile attentively, then, aside). I must try to win him over. Without his help I cannot carry it out. (Aloud.) Come this way!

№ 8. Duet.—„Jetzt, Alter, hat es Eile!"

Allegro con brio.

18108

70

18108

72

dem Staa - te liegt da - ran,
There are af - fairs of weight:

den bö - - sen Un-ter-than schnell, schnell aus dem Weg zu
A pris - -on - er of state Must, must die at once for

Clar. & Ob.

Viol.

räumen. Du stehst noch an? du stehst noch an?
treason. You would de - bate? You would de - bate?

TURN ASIDE

Rocco.

O Herr! O Herr!
My lord! My lord!

Str.

look to mirror

(aside)

Er darf nicht län - - ger le - ben, sonst ist's um mich ge-
No plan could now a - vail me, Were he a - live and

(aside)

die Glie - der fühl' ich be - ben, wie konnt' ich das be-
I fear my limbs will fail me! How could I do the

Viol.

18108

74

18108

P.
Zei-chen, dann werd' ich selbst, ver - mummt, mich in den Ker - ker
sig - nal, Then, well - dis-guis'd, I'll come, And, glid - - ing in there
Viol.
pp
Ob.
schleichen, ein Stoss! und er ver - stummt. Er
soft - ly— One blow! and he is dumb. He'll
(with the
R.
Rocco.
Ver -
To
Wind
cresc.
ff
Trb.
pp
Viol.
p
Wood wind)
sterb' in sei - - nen Ket - ten, zu kurz war sei - ne
per - - ish in his fet - ters, Too short has been his
hun - gernd in den Ket - ten, er - trug er lan - ge
starve and die in fet - ters, How long has been his
Pein! Sein Tod nur kann mich ret - ten, dann
pain! His death a - lone can save me, I
Pein, ihn töd - - ten, heisst ihn ret - ten, der
pain! To kill him is to spare him, 'Twill
cresc.
f
p
Wind
low stab
hand + drop knife
out to front

№ 9. Recitative and Aria.—„Abscheulicher! wo eilst du hin?"

Hoff- nung, lass den letz-ten Stern, den letz-ten Stern der Mü-den nicht er-
Hope, let not the on-ly star, the on-ly star_ Of sor-row be de-

blei - chen, o komm, er - hell', er-hell' mein
nied___ me, O come, light thou,___ light thou my

Ziel,_ sei's noch so fern, so fern, die Lie-be, sie wird's er-
goal,_ how-ev-er far, so far,_ And love will sure-ly

reichen, ja, ja, sie wird's er-rei -
guide me, yes, love will surely guide _____

- -chen, sie wird's er-rei -
_____ me, will sure-ly guide _____

* The original Score reads: Ossia:
- - chen, er - rei -

84

18108

86

nicht,   nein,   nein,   ich   wan - - ke
will,   with   stead - - fast,   stead - - fast

nicht,   mich stärkt die Pflicht der treu - en Gat - -
will   I   fol - low still Where wife - ly   love

- - - - - - - ten - lie - be!
may call me!

(Marzelline kommt aus dem Hause. Jaquino folgt ihr.)

Jaquino. Aber Marzelline _

Marzelline. Kein Wort, keine Silbe! Ich will nichts mehr von deinen albernen Liebesseufzern hören, dabei bleibt es.

(Enter Marcelline from house, followed by Jaquino.)

Jaquino. But Marcelline _

Marcelline. Not a word, not a syllable! I'll hear no more of your silly love-whinings _ that settles it!

18108

Jaquino. Wer das gesagt hätte, als ich mir vornahm, mich recht ordentlich in dich zu verlieben! Da war ich der gute, liebe Jaquino an allen Orten und Ecken. Aber seit dieser Fidelio _

"arzelline (rasch einfallend.) Ich leugne nicht, ich war dir gut, aber sieh', ich bin offenherzig, das war keine Liebe. Fidelio zieht mich weit mehr an, zwischen ihm und mir fühle ich eine weit grössere Übereinstimmung.

Jaquino. Eine Übereinstimmung mit einem solchen hergelaufenen Jungen, den der Vater aus blossem Mitleid am Thor dort aufgelesen hat, der _ der _

"arzelline (ärgerlich.) Der arm und verlassen ist _ und den ich doch heirathe.

Jaquino. Dass es ja nicht in meiner Gegenwart geschieht, ich möchte euch einen gewaltigen Streich spielen!

Rocco, Leonore (kommen aus dem Garten.)

Rocco. Was habt ihr beide denn wieder zu zanken?

"arzelline. Ach, Vater, er verfolgt mich immer.

Rocco. Warum denn?

"arzelline. Er will, dass ich ihn lieben, dass ich ihn heirathen soll.

Jaquino. Wenn sie mich nicht liebt, so soll sie mich wenigstens heirathen.

Rocco. Still! (Er blickt lachend auf Jaquino.) Nein, Jaquino, von deiner Heirath ist jetzt keine Rede, mich beschäftigen andere, klügere Absichten.

"arzelline. Ich verstehe, Vater. (Zärtlich leise) Fidelio!

Leonore. Brechen wir davon ab. _ Rocco, ich ersuchte Euch schon einige Male, die armen Gefangenen, die hier über der Erde wohnen, in unsern Festungsgarten zu lassen. Ihr verspracht und verschobt es immer. Heute ist das Wetter so schön, der Gouverneur kommt um diese Zeit nicht hierher.

"arzelline. O ja! ich bitte mit ihm!

Rocco. Kinder, ohne Erlaubniss des Gouverneurs!

"arzelline. Aber er sprach so lange mit dir. Vielleicht sollst du ihm einen Gefallen thun und dann wird er es so genau nicht nehmen.

Rocco. Einen Gefallen! Du hast Recht, Marzelline. Auf diese Gefahr hin kann ich es wagen. Wohl denn, Jaquino und Fidelio, öffnet die leichteren Gefängnisse. Ich aber gehe zu Pizarro und halte ihn zurück, indem ich (zu Marzelline) für dein Bestes rede.

"arzelline (küsst ihm die Hand.) So recht, Vater!

Rocco (ab durch den Schlosseingang.) Jaquino (holt aus seinem Stübchen die Schlüssel.) Leonore (öffnet mit Jaquino die Gefängnissthüren und geht dann in Roccos Wohnung ab.) Jaquino, Marzelline (ab durch den Schlosseingang.)

18108

Jaquino. Who would have thought it, when I made up my mind to fall downright in love with you! Then I was "dear, good Jaquino" here, there and everywhere! But since this Fidelio _

Marcelline (hastily interrupting). I won't deny that I liked you; but see, to be open with you, that was not love! Fidelio attracts me far more; between him and me I feel a much greater congeniality.

Jaquino. Congeniality _ with such a young vagabond, that your father picked up by the gate from pure pity, that _ that _

Marcelline (vexed). That is poor and forsaken _ and that I shall marry for all that!

Jaquino. Don't let it happen in my presence _ I might do something you'd be eternally sorry for!

(Enter Rocco and Leonora from garden.)

Rocco. What are you two quarreling about again?

Marcelline. Oh, Father, he is after me all the time!

Rocco. What for?

Marcelline. He wants me to love him _ to marry him.

Jaquino. If she doesn't love me, at least she might marry me!

Rocco. Hush! (Looking at Jaquino with a smile.) No, Jaquino, we shall waste no more words about your marriage; I am occupied with other and more sensible projects.

Marcelline. I understand, Father. (Low and fondly.) Fidelio!

Leonora. Let us change the subject. _ Rocco, I have already begged you several times to allow the poor prisoners, who dwell here aboveground, to walk in our garden. You have always promised, and put it off. To-day the weather is so lovely, and the Overseer does not come to us at this hour.

Marcelline. O yes! I beg you, too!

Rocco. Children! without the Overseer's permission!

Marcelline. But he was talking with you so long: perhaps he wants you to do him a favor, and then he would not be so very particular.

Rocco. A favor! You are right, Marcelline; now I think of that, I can take the risk. Good; Jaquino and Fidelio, open the cells aboveground. Meantime I shall go to Pizarro and keep him away, while persuading him for your benefit (to Marcelline).

Marcelline (kissing his hand). That is right, Father!

(Exit Rocco through the castle gate. Jaquino fetches the keys from his room. Leonora helps him unlock the prison-doors, then exit into Rocco's house. Exeunt Jaquino and Marcelline through the castle gate.)

№ 10. Finale.-Chorus:-„O welche Lust!"

Tenor Solo (sung by one or several).

Wir wol - len mit Ver-trauen auf Got - tes
Our trust - ful hearts per-suade us To bear till

pp

R. frei'n, — er muss in ei - ner Stun-de_den Finger auf dem Munde_ von uns be -
how! He must be bur-ied_ hark you, No word to an - y, mark you! Within an

Leonora.

(shrinking back)

L. So ist er todt? Ist, ihn zu
Then he is dead? But are you

R. gra - ben sein. Noch nicht, noch nicht!
hour from now. Not yet, not yet!

Str. & W. Wind

mf *p*

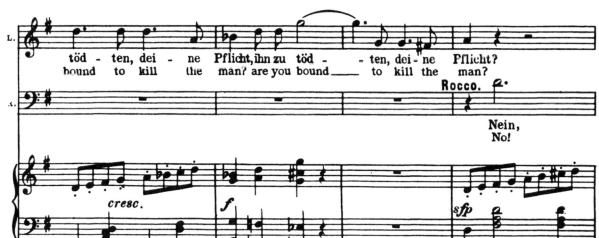

L. töd - ten, dei - ne Pflicht, ihn zu töd - - ten, dei - ne Pflicht?
bound to kill the man? are you bound____ to kill the man?

Rocco.

Nein,
No!

cresc. *f* *sfp*
sfp

R. gu-ter Jun-ge, zittre nicht! zum Morden, zum Mor - den dingt sich
my dear fel-low, never fret! No murder, no mur-der I will

sfp *sfp* *sfp* *f*
sfp *sfp* *sfp*

18108

R.

Roc-co nicht, nein, nein, nein, nein, nein, nein! Der Gouver - neur, ___ der Gou-ver-
do, nor can! No, no, no, no, no, no! The O - ver - seer ___ him-self will

sf *sf* *sf* *sf*

Viol.

R.

neur kommt selbst hin - ab, wir bei-de gra-ben nur das
meet us in the cave, We two must on-ly dig the

Str. & Tromb.

fp

Leonora (aside).

L.

Vielleicht das Grab des Gat - ten graben,
May-be the grave of him ___ I cherish,

R.

Grab. Ich darf ihn nicht mit Spei-se la-ben,
grave. For him 'tis bet-ter so to per-ish,

W. Wind.

cresc. *p*

L.

was kann fürch -ter-li - cher sein, was kann
What a dread -ful deed is there! what a

R.

ihm wird im Gra-be besser sein, ihm wird im
To give him food I do not dare, to give him

cresc. *decresc.* *p*

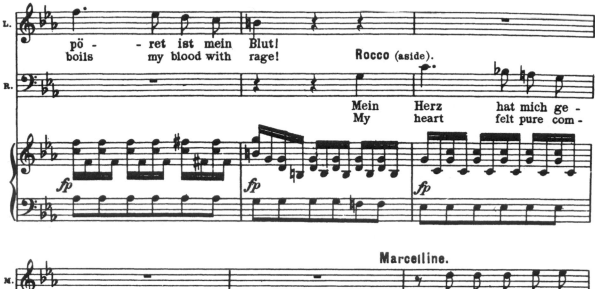

pö - - ret ist mein Blut!
boils my blood with rage!

Rocco (aside).

Mein Herz hat mich ge -
My heart felt pure com -

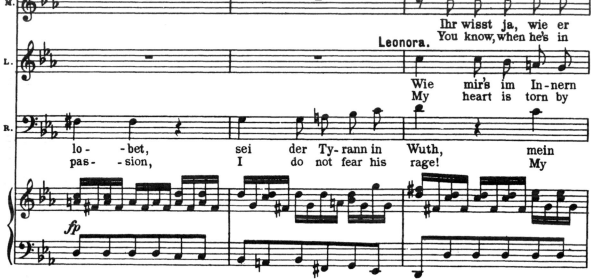

Marcelline.

Ihr wisst ja, wie er
You know, when he's in

Leonora.

Wie mir's im In - nern
My heart is torn by

lo - - bet, sei der Ty - rann in Wuth, mein
pas - - sion, I do not fear his rage! My

to - - bet, und ken-net sei - ne Wuth, Ihr wisst ja, wie er
pas - - sion, How wild-ly he can rage, You know, when he's in

to - - bet! Em - pö - ret ist mein Blut, em -
pas - - sion, And boils my blood with rage! and

Herz hat mich ge - lo - - bet, sei der Ty - rann in
heart felt pure com - pas - - sion, I do not fear his

(She hastens after Jaquino.)

M. to - bet, und ken - net sei - - ne Wuth.
pas - sion, How wild - ly he can rage!

L. pö - ret, ja, em - pö - ret ist mein Blut!
boils my blood, and boils my blood with rage!

(Enter Pizarro, with Officers, through the castle gate.)

R. Wuth, sei der Ty-rann in Wuth!
rage, I do not fear his rage!

sfp cresc. *ff* Tutti

Pizarro.

P. Ver - weg' - - - - - - - ner old
You mad - - - - - - - -

P. Al - - ter! wel - che Rech - - - te legst du dir
fel - - low! who en - gag - - - es You for a

sf *sf*

P. fre - velnd sel - ber bei? und ziemt es dem ge - dung' - nen Knechte, zu geben
place you can - not fill? What right has one who serves for wag - es To let the

sf *marcato*

18108

die Gefang'nen frei? **Rocco** (abashed). Wohl - an! Wohl-an!
pris'ners out at will? Speak out! speak out!

O Herr! O Herr!
My lord — my lord!

Rocco (seeking an excuse).

Des Früh - lings Kom - men, das hei - tre, war-me
This spring - -tide sea - son — The sun - ny day, so

(growing bolder)

Son-nen - licht, ... dann ... habt Ihr wohl in Acht ge-nommen, was sonst zu
warm and clear — Then — You must know the oth - er rea-son That tells to

(doffing his cap)

mei-nem Vor - theil spricht? Des Kö - nigs Na - mens -
my ad - van-tage here! This day's our King's, for

(aside to

fest ist heu-te, das fei-ern wir auf sol-che Art, auf sol-che Art. Der
'tis his nameday, That is the day we hon-or so, we hon-or so. Down

Pizarro)

un-ten stirbt, doch lasst die an-dern jetzt fröh-lich hin und wie-der
there, he'll die: so let his fel-lows Stroll where the sunshine cheers and

Pizarro (sotto voce).

So ei-le, ihm sein
Be off, then, dig his

wan-dern; für Je-nen sei der Zorn ge-spart.
mel-lows, And spare your rage for him be-low.

Grab zu graben, hier will ich stil-le Ru-he ha-ben; schliess' die Ge-fäng'nen
grave in haste! Here and to-day I will have rest! Now lock the pris'ners

18108

Chorus of Prisoners. (Reënter Jaquino and Marcelline from the garden.)

Allegretto vivace.

Tenor I & II.

Leb' wohl, du war-mes Son-nen-licht, schnell schwindest du uns wie-der, schnell
Fare-well, O sun-shine warm and bright, Too soon art thou de-part-ed, too

Bass I & II.

Leb' wohl, du war-mes Son-nen-licht, schnell schwindest du uns wie-der, schnell
Fare-well, O sun-shine warm and bright, Too soon art thou de-part-ed, too

Allegretto vivace.

Marcelline (gazing on the Prisoners).

Wie eil - ten sie zum Sonnenlicht,
How glad they were to hail the light,

Leonora (to the Prisoners).

Ihr hört das Wort, drum zö-gert nicht,
He or - ders you to leave the light,

Jaquino (to the Prisoners).

Ihr hört das Wort, drum zö-gert nicht,
He or - ders you to leave the light,

Pizarro.

Rocco.

Nun, Roc - -co, zög-re län-ger
Now, Roc - -co, down to yon-der

Chorus.

Nein,
My

schwindest du uns wie-der, leb' wohl, leb' wohl, du
soon art thou de-part-ed! Fare-well, fare-well, O

schwindest du uns wie-der, leb' wohl, leb' wohl, du
soon art thou de-part-ed! Fare-well, fare-well, O

M.
L.
J.
P.
R.
Tutti
cresc.
f
schei - den trau - - rig wie - der, wie eil - ten sie zum
now so heav- - - y - heart - ed! How glad they were to
in den Ker- - - ker wie- - der, ihr hört das Wort, drum
for your cells be start - ed! He or - ders you to
Ker-ker wie-der, ihr hört das Wort, das Wort, drum zö - gert,
cells be start-ed! He or-ders you to leave the light, to
nie-der, zög- - - re nicht, nun, Roc - co, zög-re län-ger,
start-ed! down to yon-der wight, now, Rocco, down to
ich stei-ge ei - lend nie-der, nein, Herr, ich zög - re län - ger,
I know 'tis time I start-ed, my lord, I'll work with all my
schnell schwindest du uns wie - - der, du war - mes Son - - - - nen - -
Too soon art thou de - part - ed, O sun - shine warm and
Son - - nen - licht, wie eil - ten sie zum Son - nen - licht, und
hail the light, how glad they were to hail the light, And
zö - - gert nicht, ihr hört das Wort, drum zö - gert nicht, kehrt
leave the light, he or - ders you to leave the light, Now
zö - - gert nicht, ihr hört das Wort, drum zö - gert nicht, kehrt
leave the light, he or - ders you to leave the light, Now
zög - re nicht, zög - re, zög - re län - ger, län - ger nicht, steig'
yon - der wight, down to yon - der wight, to yon - der wight, High
län - - ger nicht, nein, Herr, ich zög - - re län - ger nicht, ich
might, my lord, I'll work, with all, with all my might, I
licht, du war - - - - - mes Son - nen - licht, schnell
bright, O sun - - - - shine warm and bright, too

M.
Die An-dern, die An-dern murmeln nie-der, hier wohnt die
They're murm'ring, they're murm'ring down, well-guarded: Here is no
L.
Angst rinnt durch mei-ne Glie-der, er-eilt den Frev-ler, den
Dread to my soul has dart-ed, Shall Heav'n this wan-ton, this
J.
Sie sin-nen auf und nie-der,
Their words are low and guard-ed:
P.
wie-der, bis ich voll-zo-gen das Ge-richt, bis ich voll
part-ed, Till he has felt my pow'r to smite, till he has
R.
un-glück-se-lig har-te Pflicht, o un-glück-
du-ty fills my soul with fright, this du-ty
sinkt die Nacht her-nie-der, aus
soon will be de-part-ed, How
Viol.
fp
fp
fp
cresc.
M.
Lust, die Freu-de nicht, hier wohnt die Lust, die Freu-de, die
joy, is no de-light, here is no joy, no joy, here is
L.
Frev-ler kein Ge-richt, er-eilt den Frev-ler kein Ge-
wan-ton wretch not smite, shall Heav'n this wan-ton wretch not
J.
könnt' ich ver-stehn, was je-der spricht!
Could I but catch them in their flight!
P.
zo-gen das Ge-richt, nicht e-her kehrst du
felt my pow'r to smite! You two will not be
R.
se-lig har-te Pflicht!
fills my soul with fright!
der so bald kein Mor-gen bricht,
long 'twill be ere morn-ing light,
Str.
W. Wind
fp
p
Horns

M. Lust, die Freu_de, die Freu - - - - de nicht.
joy, no joy, here is no de - - light.

L. kein Ge - richt, _____ den Frev - ler!
Heav'n not smite, _____ not smite him!

J. was Je - der spricht, was Je - der spricht, was Je - der spricht!
could I but catch, could I but catch them in their flight!

P. das Ge - richt, bis ich voll - zo - gen das Ge - richt.
pow'r to smite, till he has felt my pow'r to smite!

R. har - te, har - - - te Pflicht!
fills my soul with fright!

bald kein Mor - - - - gen bricht.
long till morn - - - - ing light!

(The Prisoners return to their cells, which Leonora and Jaquino lock up.)

bald kein Mor - - - - gen bricht.
long till morn - - - - ing light!

End of Act I.

Leonore.
Overture № 3.
(Composed 1806.)

Allegro.

130

13108

18108

18108

18108

Presto.

18108

ACT II.

Dark, subterranean dungeon.

№ 11. Introduction and Aria.—„Gott! welch' Dunkel hier!"

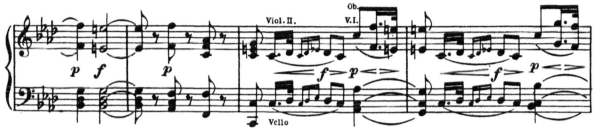

Recit. **Florestan** (seated on a

Gott!___ welch Dun-kel
God!___ what gloom is

stone, with a long chain about his body).

hier!
here!

O grauen-vol-le Stil-le!
O silence, full of terror!

Öd' ist es um mich her,
Lone-ly as in my grave,

nichts, nichts le - bet ausser
Ah! no liv - ing soul is

Poco allegro.

Ob. Solo (highest part)

p Str. & Horns   *cresc.* - - - - - - - - - *dimin.*

Florestan (with an exaltation akin to madness, tho' outwardly tranquil).

Und spür' ich nicht lin-de, sanft säuselnde Luft?   und ist nicht mein
And are not soft breezes ca-ressing me here?   Is there not a

p dolce

Grab mir er-hellet?   Ich seh', wie ein Engel im ro-si-gen Duft sich tröstend zur
light in my prison?   I see how an angel in ra-di-ant air All smiling be-

cresc. - - - - - - - - *p*

Sei-te, zur Sei-te mir stellet,   ein Engel, Le-o-no-ren,   Le-o-
side me, be-side me has ris-en: An angel, Le-o-no-ra,   Le-o-

noren, der Gattin so gleich, der, der führt mich zur Freiheit in's himm - - lische
nora, the wife I a-dore, She, she leads me to freedom, where pain — — is no

cresc. poco a poco - - - - - - *f*   Viol.

18108

Reich.
more.

Und spür'ich nicht lin-de, sanft säu-seln-de Luft?
And are not soft breezes ca-ress-ing me here?

Ich seh', wie ein Engel im ro-si-gen Duft, ein Engel, ein Engel sich
I see how an angel in ra-di-ant air, an angel, an angel All

tröstend zur Sei-te mir stellet, ein Engel, Le-o-no-ren, Le-o-
smiling be-side me has risen: An angel, Le-o-no-ra, Le-o-

no-ren, der Gat-tin so gleich, der, der führt mich zur Frei-heit, zur
no-ra, the wife I a-dore, She, she leads me to free-dom, to

Frei-heit in's himm-li-sche Reich, zur Frei-heit, zur
free-dom, where pain is no more, to free-dom, to

*) Other editions:

säu-seln-de Luft?

18108

Nº 12. Melodrama and Duet.

(Rocco and Leonora, descending the stairway by the light of a lantern, carrying a pitcher and the tools for digging.)

Wir brauchen nicht viel zu graben,
um an die Öffnung zu kommen; gieb
mir eine Haue und du, stelle dich hie-
her. (Steigt bis an den Gürtel in die
Höhlung, stellt den Krug neben sich. Leonore reicht ihm die Haue.)

We need not dig far to reach the
opening; give me a pickaxe, and
come and stand here. (Descends in
the cavity up to his waist, setting the
pitcher down near him. Leonora hands
him a pickaxe.)

Du zitterst,
You tremble.

Allegro.

fürchtest du dich?
are you afraid?

Str.

Leonore. O nein, es ist nur
so kalt.
Rocco (rasch). So mache fort,
im Arbeiten wird dir schon
warm werden.
Leonora. Oh no! only it is
so cold.
Rocco (quickly). Then get
to work; working will make
you warm enough.

Andantino.

Duet. — „Nur hurtig fort, nur frisch gegraben."

(Rocco, as the ritornello begins, commences to work; meantime Leonora employs the moments when Rocco
bends down, to observe the prisoner.)

Andante con moto.

Str. pp

Wind, w. Tromb. & Doub.- Bssn.

fp

Rocco (sotto voce, while at work).

Nur hurtig   fort, nur frisch ge -
Now work a - way, we must be

fp   decresc.   pp

154

(aside, trying to get a view of the prisoner)

18108

156

18108

Rocco (trinkt.) Florestan (erholt sich und hebt das Haupt in die Höhe, ohne sich nach Leonore zu wenden.)

Leonore. Er erwacht!

Rocco (plötzlich im Trinken einhaltend.) Er erwacht, sagst du?

Leonore (in grösster Verwirrung immer nach Florestan sehend.) Ja, er hat eben den Kopf in die Höhe gehoben.

Rocco. Ohne Zweifel wird er wieder tausend Fragen an mich stellen. Ich muss allein mit ihm reden. (Er steigt aus der Grube.) Steig' du statt meiner hinab und räume noch so viel hinweg, dass man die Cisterne leicht öffnen kann.

Leonore (steigt zitternd einige Stufen hinab.) Was in mir vorgeht, ist unaussprechlich!

Rocco (zu Florestan) Nun, Ihr habt wieder einige Augenblicke geruht?

Florestan. Geruht? Wie fände ich Ruhe?

Leonore (für sich.) Diese Stimme! — Wenn ich nur einen Augenblick sein Gesicht sehen könnte!

Florestan. Werdet Ihr immer bei meinen Klagen taub sein, harter Mann? (Bei den letzten Worten wendet er sein Gesicht gegen Leonore.)

Leonore (für sich.) Gott! Er ist's. (Sie fällt bewusstlos an den Rand der Grube.)

Rocco. Was verlangt Ihr denn von mir? Ich vollziehe die Befehle, die man mir giebt; das ist mein Amt, meine Pflicht.

Florestan. Sagt mir endlich einmal, wer ist Gouverneur dieses Gefängnisses.

Rocco (bei Seite) Jetzt kann ich's ihm ja ohne Gefahr sagen. (Zu Florestan) Der Gouverneur dieses Gefängnisses ist Don Pizarro.

Florestan. Pizarro! Er ist es, dessen Verbrechen ich zu entdecken wagte.

Leonore (sich allmählich erholend, bei Seite.) O Barbar! Deine Grausamkeit giebt mir meine Kräfte wieder.

Florestan. O schickt so bald als möglich nach Sevilla, fragt nach Leonore Florestan —

Leonore (bei Seite.) Gott! Er ahnt nicht, dass sie jetzt sein Grab gräbt.

Florestan. Sagt ihr, dass ich hier in Ketten liege.

Rocco. Es ist unmöglich, sag' ich Euch. Ich würde mich in's Verderben stürzen, ohne Euch genützt zu haben.

Florestan. Wenn ich denn verdammt bin, hier mein Leben zu enden, o so lasst mich nicht langsam verschmachten.

(Rocco takes a draught. Florestan comes to himself and raises his head, without turning towards Leonora.)

Leonora. He is waking!

Rocco (stops short in drinking). He is waking, you say?

Leonora (in extreme agitation, gazing fixedly at Florestan). Yes, he just raised his head.

Rocco. No doubt he'll have a thousand questions to ask me, as usual. I must talk with him alone. (Climbs out of the hole.) Get down now where I was and clear away enough, so that we can easily open the well.

Leonora (descends a few steps, trembling). No words can tell what I feel!

Rocco (to Florestan). Well, it seems you have rested again a few moments.

Florestan. Rested! How should I find rest?

Leonora (aside). That voice! If I could only see his face for an instant.

Florestan. Will you always be deaf to my complaints, you man of stone? (While speaking, he turns his face towards Leonora.)

Leonora (aside). My God! it is he! (Falls swooning on the edge of the cavity.)

Rocco. What would you have me do? I carry out the orders that are given me; that is my office — my duty.

Florestan. Do tell me, at last, who the overseer of this prison is.

Rocco (aside). I can tell him now, without risk. (To Florestan): The overseer of this prison is Don Pizarro.

Florestan. Pizarro! the very man whose crimes I dared bring to light!

Leonora (gradually coming to herself; aside). Oh, you tyrant! Your cruelty renews my strength.

Florestan. Oh, send as soon as possible to Seville, inquire for Leonora Florestan —

Leonora (aside). Heavens! He little imagines that she is digging his grave!

Florestan. Tell her that I am lying here in chains.

Rocco. It is impossible, I tell you. I should only ruin myself, without doing you any good.

Florestan. If I am indeed condemned to end my life here, do not let me perish by slow starvation.

Leonore (springt auf und hält sich an der Mauer; bei Seite.) O Gott! Wer kann das ertragen?

Florestan. Aus Barmherzigkeit, gebt mir nur einen Tropfen Wasser. Das ist ja so wenig—

Rocco (bei Seite.) Es geht mir wider meinen Willen zu Herzen—

Leonore (bei Seite.) Er scheint sich zu erweichen.

Florestan. Du giebst mir keine Antwort?

Rocco. Ich kann Euch nicht verschaffen, was Ihr verlangt. Alles, was ich Euch anbieten kann, ist ein Restchen Wein, das ich in meinem Krug habe.— Fidelio!

Leonore (den Krug in grösster Eile bringend.) Da ist er. Da ist er!

Florestan (Leonore betrachtend.) Wer ist das?

Rocco. Mein Schliesser und in wenig Tagen mein Eidam. (Er reicht Florestan den Krug. Dieser trinkt.) Es ist freilich nur ein wenig Wein, aber ich gebe ihn Euch gern. (Zu Leonore.) Du bist ganz in Bewegung?

Leonore (in grösster Verwirrung.) Wer sollte es nicht sein? Ihr selbst, Meister Rocco...

Rocco. Es ist wahr, der Mensch hat so eine Stimme...

Leonore. Ja wohl, sie dringt in die Tiefe des Herzens.

Leonora (springing up and leaning on the wall; aside). My God! who can bear to hear him?

Florestan. Have pity on me, give me only one drop of water; that is so little.

Rocco (aside). It goes to my heart in spite of me.

Leonora (aside). He seems to be touched.

Florestan. You give me no answer?

Rocco. I cannot give you what you ask for. All that I can offer you is a trifle of wine I have left in my pitcher. _ Fidelio!

Leonora (bringing the pitcher in the greatest haste). Here it is! Here it is!

Florestan (looking at Leonora). Who is this?

Rocco. My turnkey, in a few days to be my son-in-law. (He hands the pitcher to Florestan, who drinks.) To be sure, it's only a drop of wine, but I'm glad to give it you. (To Leonora.) You are quite agitated.

Leonora (in the utmost agitation). Who could help it? You yourself, Master Rocco—

Rocco. It is true, the man has such a voice—

Leonora. Ah, it goes to the very depths of the heart!

№ 13. Trio. _ „Euch werde Lohn in bessern Welten.“

160

18108

L. ar-mer, du ar-mer Mann, du armer, du ar-mer Mann!
suff'rer, poor suff'rer you, poor suff'rer, poor suff'rer you!

Flor. (seizing Leonora's hand).
O Dank dir, Dank, o
How can I tell my

F. Dank, o Dank! o Dank! my thanks! Euch, euch
thanks, how tell my thanks! Oh, may

cresc. sfp cresc. Viol. p Clar. & Bssn. cresc. Str.

Leonora.
L. Der Him-mel
Pray Heav'n may

F. wer - de Lohn in bes - sern Wel-ten, der Him-mel
Heav'n's own grace re - ward you — du - ly, Whose mer - cy

Rocco.
R. Mich rühr - te
Tho' I was

Viol. p W.W.

L. schi - - cke Ret - - tung — dir, — dann
send you help in — need, — Then

F. hat — euch mir, euch mir ge - schickt, o Dank!
sent — you, sent you to my cell! O thanks!

R. oft — dein Lei - den hier, doch
oft - - en moved, in - deed, I

wird mir ho - her Lohn, _____ mir ho - her Lohn ge-
I shall reap re - ward, _____ shall reap my full re -

o Dank! der Him - mel hat euch mir ge-
O thanks! 'Twas Heav'n that sent you to my

Hül - - fe, doch Hül - - fe war mir streng ver -
nev - - er, I nev - - er dared of - fend my

währt, dann wird mir ho - her, ho - her Lohn ge - währt.
ward, _____ then I shall reap, shall reap my full re - ward.

schickt, o Dank! o Dank! Ihr habt mich süss er - quickt. Bewegt seh'
cell! O thanks! O thanks! You have refreshed me well! Howmoved this

wehrt, doch Hül - fe, Hül - fe war mir streng, streng ver-wehrt. Ich labt' ihn
lord, but nev - er dared, but nev - er dared of-fend my lord! Poor man, I'm

*)

cresc.

mf Wind

sf

p Str.

Ihr labt' ihn gern, den ar - men Mann,den ar - men,
How glad you were to help him, too! Howglad you

ich den Jüng - ling hier, und Rührung zeigt auch die - ser Mann,
youth ap - pears to be, And this man's eyes, me-thought,were wet:

gern, den ar - men Mann, es ist ja bald um ihn ge - than,den ar - men,
glad I did un - bend, For, af - ter all, he's near his end, for, af - ter

Fl. & Viol.

Clar., Bssn.

*) In other Editions: b instead of g♯

Rocco (nach augenblicklichem Stillschweigen zu Leonore.) Alles ist bereit. Ich gehe, das Signal zu geben.

(Er geht in den Hintergrund.)

Leonore. O Gott, gieb mir Muth und Stärke.

Florestan (zu Leonore, während Rocco die Thür zu öffnen geht.) Wo geht er hin?

(Rocco öffnet die Thür und giebt durch einen starken Pfiff das Zeichen.)

Florestan. Ist das der Vorbote meines Todes?

Leonore (in heftiger Bewegung.) Nein, nein! Beruhige dich, lieber Gefangener.

Florestan. O meine Leonore! So soll ich dich nie wieder sehen!

Leonore (fühlt sich zu Florestan hingerissen und sucht diesen Trieb zu überwältigen.) Mein ganzes Herz reisst mich zu ihm hin! (Zu Florestan.) Sei ruhig, sag' ich dir! Was du auch hören und sehen magst, vergiss nicht, dass überall eine Vorsehung herrscht. — Ja, es giebt eine Vorsehung! (Sie entfernt sich und geht gegen die Cisterne.)

Pizarro (kommt in einem Mantel gehüllt, halblaut zu Rocco, die Stimme verstellend.) Ist alles bereit?

Rocco (halb laut.) Ja, die Cisterne braucht nur geöffnet zu werden.

Pizarro (ebenso.) Gut, der Bursche soll sich entfernen.

Rocco (zu Leonore.) Geh', entferne dich!

Leonore (in grösster Verwirrung.) Wer?_Ich?_ Und Ihr?

Rocco. Muss ich nicht dem Gefangenen die Eisen abnehmen? Geh'! geh'!

(Leonore zieht sich in den Hintergrund zurück, nähert sich aber allmählig wieder im Schatten, die Augen immer auf Pizarro gerichtet.)

Pizarro (bei Seite.) Die muss ich mir noch heute beide vom Halse schaffen, damit alles auf immer verborgen bleibt.

Rocco (zu Pizarro.) Soll ich ihm die Ketten abnehmen?

Pizarro. Nein, aber schliesse ihn von dem Stein los. (bei Seite.) Die Zeit ist dringend. (Er zieht einen Dolch. Rocco vollzieht Pizarros Befehl.)

Rocco (to Leonora, after a moment of silence). Everything is ready. I am going to give the signal.

(Goes to back.)

Leonora. Oh God, give me strength and courage!

Florestan (to Leonora, as Rocco is going to open the door). Where is he going?

(Rocco opens door, and gives the signal by a shrill whistle.)

Florestan. Is that the signal for my death?

Leonora (extremely agitated). No, no! Calm yourself, dear prisoner.

Florestan. O my Leonora! Shall I never see you again?

Leonora (feeling herself overpoweringly drawn to Florestan, and seeking to resist the impulse). My whole heart impels me to him! (To Florestan.) Be calm, I tell you! Whatever you may hear or see, do not forget that Providence rules over all. — Yes, there is a Providence! (She retires towards the well.)

Pizarro (enters, disguised by a long cloak; in an undertone to Rocco, with a feigned voice). Is everything ready?

Rocco (in an undertone). Yes, the well need only be opened.

Pizarro (as before). Good; now let the boy leave us.

Rocco (to Leonora). Now go; you must leave us.

Leonora (in great confusion). Who? I?_ And you?

Rocco. Must I not take off the prisoner's chains? Go! go!

(Leonora withdraws to the back, but then comes forward again gradually in the shadows, her eyes intently fixed on Pizarro.)

Pizarro (aside). I must get rid of those two this very day, so that nothing may ever come to light.

Rocco (to Pizarro). Shall I take off his chains?

Pizarro. No, but unchain him from the stone. (Aside.) Time presses. (Draws a dagger. Rocco carries out Pizarro's order.)

№14. Quartet. — „Er sterbe!"

178

18108

(The trumpet sounds more loudly. Jaquino, officers and soldiers appear on the stairway with torches.)

Jaquino. Vater Rocco, der Herr Minister kommt an, sein Gefolge ist schon vor dem Schlossthor.

Rocco (freudig und überrascht, für sich.) Gelobt sei Gott! (sehr laut.) Wir kommen, ja wir kommen augenblicklich, und diese Leute mit Fackeln sollen heruntersteigen und den Herrn Gouverneur hinaufbegleiten.

Jaquino. Father Rocco, his lordship the Minister is coming; his train is already at the castle gate.

Rocco (with delighted surprise; aside). God be praised! (Very loud.) We are coming, we are coming immediately; let the men with torches come down and accompany the Lord Overseer upstairs!

*) In other editions: Bunde

Presto.

Mu - the dich be - freih.—
love, shall set thee free! —

Mu - the mich be - - freih.
love, shall set me free!

mei - ner Ra - che sein.
ven - geance that should be!

die - sem Wüth'- rich sein.
this vile wretch I'll be!

(Pizarro rushes off, making Rocco a sign to follow him. The latter seizes the hands of both spouses, presses them to his breast, points up to heaven, and hastens after. The soldiers precede him.)

Presto.

ff Tutti (without Tromb.)

Florestan. O meine Leonore!	**Florestan.** O my Leonora!
Leonore. Florestan!	**Leonora.** Florestan!
Florestan. Was hast du für mich gethan?	**Florestan.** What have you done for me?
Leonore. Nichts, mein Florestan!	**Leonora.** Nothing, my Florestan!

№ 15. Duet.-„O namenlose Freude."

★ In other Editions: *g*.

18108

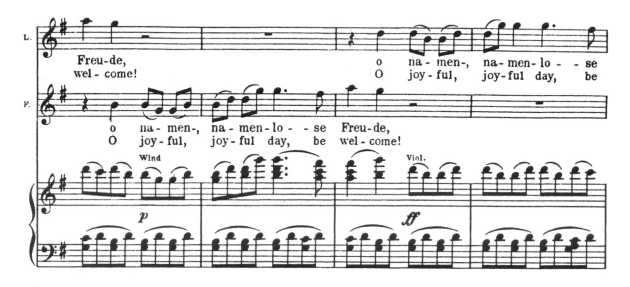

★ In other Editions: *c* instead of *b*.

№ 16. Finale.- Chorus „Heil sei dem Tag."

Bastion before the castie.

Allegro vivace.

(The Guards of the castle form a hollow square, surrounding the prisoners. Jaquino, Marcelline. Outside, populace assembled in haste. Enter through the castle gate the Minister Don Fernando, Pizarro, Officers. As the Minister appears, the prisoners fall on their knees.)

Soprano.
Heil! Heil! Heil sei dem Tag,
Hail! Hail! Hail to the day,

Alto.
Heil! Heil! Heil sei dem Tag,
Hail! Hail! Hail to the day,

Chorus of People.

Tenor.
Heil! Heil! Heil sei dem Tag,
Hail! Hail! Hail to the day,

Bass.
Heil! Heil! Heil sei dem Tag,
Hail! Hail! Hail to the day,

Tenor.
Heil! Heil! Heil sei dem Tag,
Hail! Hail! Hail to the day,

Chorus of Prisoners.

Bass.
Heil! Heil! Heil sei dem Tag,
Hail! Hail! Hail to the day,

Heil sei der Stun-de, die lang' er-sehnt, doch un-ver-meint, Ge-rech-tig-keit mit
hail to the hour So long de-sired thro' hope-less years! The sun of grace and

Heil sei der Stun-de, die lang' er-sehnt, doch un-ver-meint, Ge-rech-tig-keit mit
hail to the hour So long de-sired thro' hope-less years! The sun of grace and

Heil sei der Stun-de, die lang' er-sehnt, doch un-ver-meint, Ge-rech-tig-keit mit
hail to the hour So long de-sired thro' hope-less years! The sun of grace and

Heil sei der Stun-de, die lang' er-sehnt, doch un-ver-meint, Ge-rech-tig-keit mit
hail to the hour So long de-sired thro' hope-less years! The sun of grace and

Heil sei der Stun-de, die lang' er-sehnt, doch un-ver-meint, Ge-
hail to the hour So long de-sired thro' hope-less years! The

Heil sei der Stun-de, die lang' er-sehnt, doch un-ver-meint, Ge-
hail to the hour So long de-sired thro' hope-less years! The

Huld im Bun-de, mit Huld im Bun-de vor uns-res Gra-bes Thor er-scheint, vor
ret-ri-bu-tion, of ret-ri-bu-tion Be-fore our liv-ing tomb ap-pears, be-

Huld im Bun-de, mit Huld im Bun-de vor uns-res Gra-bes Thor er-scheint, vor
ret-ri-bu-tion, of ret-ri-bu-tion Be-fore our liv-ing tomb ap-pears, be-

Huld im Bun-de, mit Huld im Bun-de vor uns-res Gra-bes Thor er-scheint, vor
ret-ri-bu-tion, of ret-ri-bu-tion Be-fore our liv-ing tomb ap-pears, be-

Huld im Bun-de, mit Huld im Bun-de vor uns-res Gra-bes Thor er-scheint, vor
ret-ri-bu-tion, of ret-ri-bu-tion Be-fore our liv-ing tomb ap-pears, be-

rech-tig-keit mit Huld im Bun-de vor uns-res Gra-bes Thor er-scheint, vor
sun of grace and ret-ri-bu-tion Be-fore our liv-ing tomb ap-pears, be-

rech-tig-keit mit Huld im Bun-de vor uns-res Gra-bes Thor er-scheint, vor
sun of grace and ret-ri-bu-tion Be-fore our liv-ing tomb ap-pears, be-

Clar. Ob. Clar.
p f Tutti Bssn.
p p

Bssn. Basses

200

18108

★ Other Editions: *g* instead of *f♯*.

keit hält zum Ge - richt der Ra - che Schwert ge - zückt! Be - stra - fet sei der
nev - - er - more re - lent Un - til re - venge be won! A - way with him to

keit hält zum Ge - richt der Ra - che Schwert ge - zückt! Be - stra - fet sei der
nev - - er - more re - lent Un - til re - venge be won! A - way with him to

keit hält zum Ge - richt der Ra - che Schwert ge - zückt! Be - stra - fet sei der
nev - - er - more re - lent Un - til re - venge be won! A - way with him to

Tutti

ff

Tempo I.

Fernando (to Rocco).

Fru.

Du
You

(Pizarro, on a sign from Fernando, is led away.)

Bö - se - wicht!
pun - ish - ment!

Bö - se - wicht!
pun - ish - ment!

Bö - se - wicht!
pun - ish - ment!

Tempo I.

p Str.

Frn.

schlos - sest auf des Ed - len Grab, jetzt,
oped his tomb to light of day, Now,

Bssn.

15108

un - - aus-sprechlich süsses Glück! Ge - recht, o Gott! ist dein Ge - richt,
tongue our joy can ev-er tell! Thy will, O Lord, is just-ly wrought,

un - - aus-sprech - lich süsses Glück! Ge - recht, o Gott! ist dein Ge - richt,
tongue our joy can ev-er tell! Thy will, O Lord, is just-ly wrought,

un - - aus-sprechlich süsses Glück! Ge - recht, o Gott! ist dein Ge - richt, ist
tongue our joy can ev-er tell! Thy will, O Lord, is just-ly wrought,is

un - - aus-sprech - lich süsses Glück! Ge - recht, o Gott! ist dein Ge - richt,
tongue our joy can ev-er tell! Thy will, O Lord, is just-ly wrought,

un - - aus-sprech - lich süsses Glück! Ge-recht, o Gott! ist dein Ge - richt,
tongue our joy can ev-er tell! Thy will, O Lord, is just-ly wrought,

süsses Glück! Ge - recht, o Gott! ist dein Ge-richt, du prü-fest,
ev-er tell! Thy will, O Lord, is just-ly wrought,Thou tri - est,

süsses Glück! Ge - recht, o Gott! ist dein Ge-richt, du prü-fest,
ev-er tell! Thy will, O Lord, is just-ly wrought,Thou tri - est,

süsses Glück! Ge - recht, o Gott! ist dein Ge-richt, du prü-fest,
ev-er tell! Thy will, O Lord, is just-ly wrought,Thou tri - est,

* Other editions: *a* instead of *f*

Allegro ma non troppo.

Sopr.

Wer ein hol - des Weib er -
Ev - 'ry man will join us

Alto.

Wer ein hol - des Weib er -
Ev - 'ry man will join us

Chorus.

Tenor.

Wer ein hol - des Weib er -
Ev - 'ry man will join us

Bass.

Wer ein hol - des Weib er -
Ev - 'ry man will join us

Allegro ma non troppo. Tutti (without Trombones).

run - gen, stimm' in un - sern Ju - bel ein, stimm' in un - sern Ju - bel ein, nie,
proud - ly, Who has won a no - ble wife, who has won a no - ble wife; Ne'er,

run - gen, stimm' in un - sern Ju - bel ein, stimm' in un - sern Ju - bel ein, nie,
proud - ly, Who has won a no - ble wife, who has won a no - ble wife; Ne'er,

run - gen, stimm' in un - sern Ju - bel ein, stimm' in un - sern Ju - bel ein, nie,
proud - ly, Who has won a no - ble wife, who has won a no - ble wife; Ne'er,

run - gen, stimm' in un - sern Ju - bel ein, stimm' in un - sern Ju - bel ein, nie,
proud - ly, Who has won a no - ble wife, who has won a no - ble wife; Ne'er,

nie, nie wird es zu hoch be - sun - gen, Ret - te - rin,
ne'er, ne'er can prais - es ring too loud - ly: Hail to her,

nie, nie wird es zu hoch be - sun - gen, Ret - te - rin, Ret -
ne'er, ne'er can prais - es ring too loud - ly: Hail to her, hail

nie, nie wird es zu hoch be - sun - gen, Ret - te - rin, Ret -
ne'er, ne'er can prais - es ring too loud - ly: Hail to her, hail

nie, nie wird es zu hoch be - sun - gen, Ret - te - rin, Ret -
ne'er, ne'er can prais - es ring too loud - ly: Hail to her, hail

18108

Florestan (advancing, and indicating Leonora).

219

18108

220

18108

*) Other Editions· b instead of c.

hol - des Weib er - run - gen, stimm' in un - sern Ju - bel ein, wer ein hol - des Weib er -
man will join us proudly, Who has won a no - ble wife; Ev - 'ry man will join us
hol - des Weib er - run - gen, stimm' in un - sern Ju - bel ein, wer ein hol - des Weib er -
man will join us proudly, Who has won a no - ble wife; Ev - 'ry man will join us
hol - des Weib er - run - gen, stimm' in un - sern Ju - bel ein, wer ein hol - des Weib er -
man will join us proudly, Who has won a no - ble wife; Ev - 'ry man will join us
run - gen, stimm' in un - sern Ju - bel ein, in un - sern Ju - - bel ein.
proud - ly, Who has won a no - ble wife, has won a no - - ble wife.
run - gen, stimm' in un - sern Ju - bel ein, in un - sern Ju - - bel ein.
proud - ly, Who has won a no - ble wife, has won a no - - ble wife.
run - gen, stimm' in un - sern Ju - bel ein, in un - sern Ju - - bel ein.
proud - ly, Who has won a no - ble wife, has won a no - - ble wife.
Basses & Bssn.
sf
Nie wird es zu
Ne'er can prais - es
sf
Nie wird es zu hoch be - sun - gen, Ret - te - rin des Gat - ten sein, nie wird es zu
Ne'er can prais - es ring too loud - ly: Hail to her who saved his life! Ne'er can prais - es
Nie wird es zu
Ne'er can prais - es
Viol.
sf

hoch be-sun-gen, Ret - te-rin des Gat-ten sein, Ret - te-rin des Gat-ten sein.
ring too loud-ly: Hail to her who saved his life, hail to her who saved his life!

hoch be-sun-gen, Ret - te-rin des Gat-ten sein, Ret - te-rin des Gat-ten sein.
ring too loud-ly: Hail to her who saved his life, hail to her who saved his life!

hoch be-sun-gen, Ret - te-rin des Gat-ten sein, Ret - te-rin des Gat-ten sein.
ring too loud-ly: Hail to her who saved his life, hail to her who saved his life!

Leonora.

Lie - bend sei es hoch be - sun-gen, Flo - re-stan ist
Lov - ing ring my song, and loud-ly, Flo - re-stan is

Marcelline.

Nie wird es zu hoch be - sun-gen, Ret - te-rin des
Ne'er can prais-es ring too loud-ly: Hail to her who

Florestan.

Nie wird es zu hoch be - sun-gen, Ret - te-rin des
Ne'er can prais-es ring too loud-ly: Hail to her who

Jaquino.

Nie wird es zu hoch be - sun-gen, Ret - te-rin des
Ne'er can praises ring too loud-ly: Hail to her who

Fernando.

Nie wird es zu hoch be - sun-gen, Ret - te-rin des
Ne'er can praises ring too loud-ly: Hail to her who

Rocco.

Nie wird es zu hoch be - sun-gen, Ret - te-rin des
Ne'er can praises ring too loud-ly: Hail to her who

Wer ein hol-des Weib er - run-gen,
Ev - 'ry man will join us proudly,

Wer ein hol-des Weib er - run-gen,
Ev - 'ry man will join us proudly,

Wer ein hol-des Weib er - run-gen,
Ev - 'ry man will join us proudly,

Horns

Tutti

Horns

p dolce

f

p

Bssn.

Bssn.

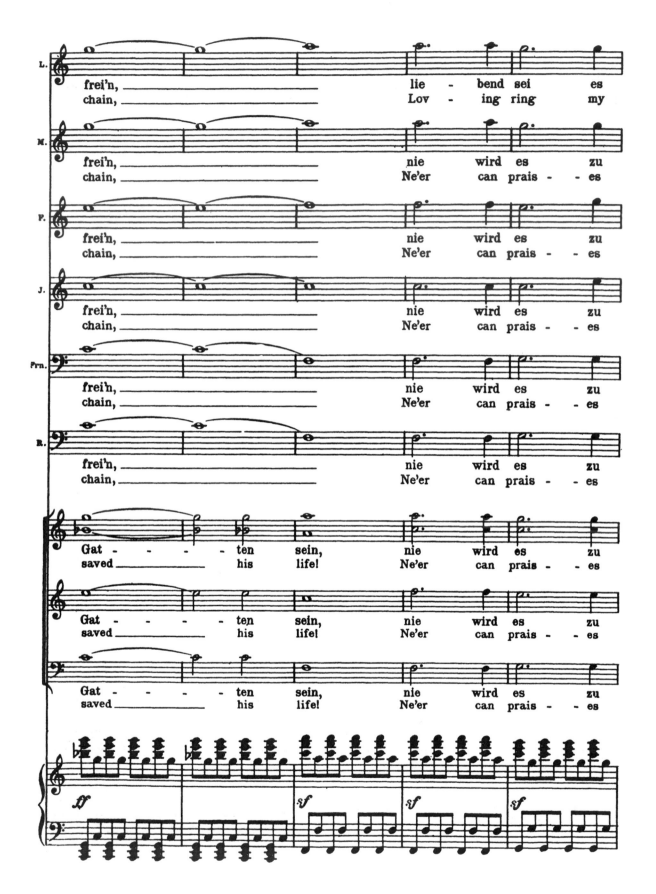

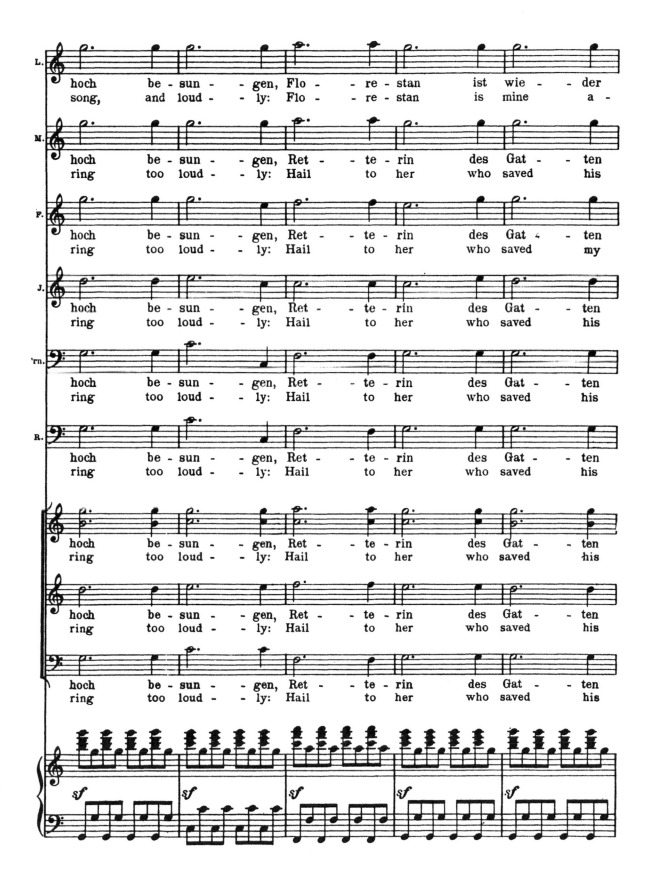

L.
mein, Flo - re - stan ist wie - der mein.
gain, Flo - re - stan is mine a - gain!

M.
sein, Ret - te - rin des Gat - ten sein.
life, hail_____ to her who saved his life!

F.
sein, Ret - te - rin des Gat - ten sein.
life, hail_____ to her who saved_____ my life!

J.
sein, Ret - te - rin des Gat - ten sein.
life, hail_____ to her who saved his life!

Prn.
sein, Ret - te - rin des Gat - ten sein.
life, hail_____ to her who saved his life!

R.
sein, Ret - te - rin des Gat - ten sein.
life, hail_____ to her who saved his life!

sein, nie wird es zu hoch be - sun-gen, Ret-te - rin des Gat-ten sein.
life, Ne'er can prais-es ring too loud-ly: Hail to her who saved his life!

sein, nie wird es zu hoch be - sun-gen, Ret-te - rin des Gat-ten sein.
life, Ne'er can prais-es ring too loud-ly: Hail to her who saved his life!

48108

End of the Opera.

Leonore.

Overture No 1.

(Composed 1807)

Allegro con brio.

Adagio ma non troppo.

Tempo I.

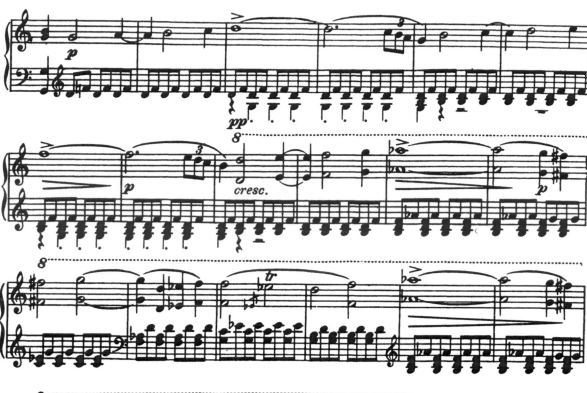

18108

Leonore.
Overture Nº 2.
(Composed 1805.)

Adagio.

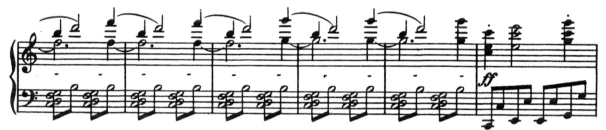

258

18108

Un poco sostenuto.

Tempo I.
p
rinf.
p
Un poco sostenuto.
Trumpet
f
p
fp
Tempo I.
pp sempre
Adagio.
p dolce
sf
p
ppp
Tempo I.
pp
cresc.

Presto.